INTRUSIVENESS AND INTIMACY IN THE COUPLE

INTRUSIVENESS AND INTIMACY IN THE COUPLE

edited by

Stanley Ruszczynski & James Fisher

Foreword by

Ronald Britton

London

KARNAC BOOKS

First published in 1995 by
H. Karnac (Books) Ltd.
58 Gloucester Road
London SW7 4QY

Cover illustration: "The Linné Family", designed by Gunnar Kanevad;
    reproduced by kind permission of Träsnideriet, Kanevad,
    Rådmansgatan 9, S-58246, Linköping, Sweden. Photograph by
    J. Fisher.

British Library Cataloguing in Publication Data

A catalogue record for this book is available from the British Library.

ISBN: 1-85575-114-3

Printed in Great Britain by BPC Wheatons Ltd, Exeter

ACKNOWLEDGEMENTS

We would like to thank the participants of the Autumn Conference of the Tavistock Marital Studies Institute held in November 1994, under the title "Projective Identification and the Couple: Intrusion? Communication?". Their enthusiastic interest in the papers presented on that occasion gave us the impetus to publish this book. Earlier versions of chapters one, two, three, and four were presented at that conference. A version of chapter one was also presented in March 1994, and versions of chapters two and four were presented in March 1995 at conferences of the Washington School of Psychiatry in Washington, D.C. Chapters five and six were prepared especially for this book.

We would also like to express our appreciation to Mr Cesare Sacerdoti of Karnac Books for his active interest in and support for the work of the Tavistock Marital Studies Institute. His encouragement has continued to play a significant role in supporting members of staff to pursue the difficult task of writing in their already busy professional schedules. We are also indebted to the skills of Klara and Eric King for their contribution, on behalf of Karnac Books, to the copyediting of the book.

CONTENTS

CONTRIBUTORS

RONALD BRITTON is a training analyst of the British Psycho-Analytical Society. He is qualified in medicine and both adult and child psychiatry and was formerly Chairman of the Department for Children and Parents at the Tavistock Clinic. Author of many important papers in psychoanalysis, including the much-cited "The Missing Link: Parental Sexuality in the Oedipus Complex", he has a new book soon to be published under the title Love, Hate and Knowledge. He is now in full-time practice.

WARREN COLMAN is a Senior Marital Psychotherapist at the TMSI and a Founder Member of the SPMP. He is an Associate Professional Member of the Society of Analytical Psychology and is in half-time private practice as a Jungian analyst.

TMSI refers to the Tavistock Marital Studies Institute, Tavistock Centre, London; SPMP stands for the Society of Psychoanalytical Marital Psychotherapists.

GIOVANNA RITA DI CEGLIE is qualified in medicine and child and adolescent psychiatry. She is a psychoanalyst of the British Psycho-Analytical Society and is in full-time private psychoanalytic practice. She is a training therapist for the Lincoln Centre and Institute for Psychotherapy.

JAMES FISHER is a Senior Marital Psychotherapist at the TMSI and a Founder Member of the SPMP. He is an Associate Member of the British Association of Psychotherapists and has a part-time private practice of psychoanalytical psychotherapy.

DONALD MELTZER is a psychoanalyst, supervisor, and teacher. He is the author of a number of books, including *The Psycho-Analytical Process* (1967), *Sexual States of Mind* (1973), *The Kleinian Development* (1978), *Dream-Life* (1983), *The Apprehension of Beauty* (with M. Harris Williams, 1988), *The Claustrum* (1992), and his collected papers, edited by Alberto Hahn, *Sincerity and Other Works* (1994).

MARY MORGAN is a Senior Marital Psychotherapist at the TMSI and a Founder Member of SPMP. She has a part-time private practice of psychoanalytical psychotherapy.

STANLEY RUSZCZYNSKI is a Senior Marital Psychotherapist at the TMSI and a Founder Member of SPMP. He is editor of *Psychotherapy with Couples* (Karnac Books, 1993). He is a Full Member of the British Association of Psychotherapists and has a part-time private practice of psychoanalytical psychotherapy.

FOREWORD

Ronald Britton

This book is timely. In our post-modern cultural, intellectual, and social scene, subjects are wafted to the surface of our collective consciousness in an unrooted way. They become briefly the focus of intense, superficial inquiry, accompanied by a flurry of activity. At the present moment, marriage—and its vicissitudes—is about to become such a subject. The crisis in "family life", or in the life of families in this country at this time, has attracted the ever-moving spotlight of the media and even the grudging attention of government. After a generation of sociological deconstruction, "post-sixties" antinomian rhetoric, and economic neglect, the family remains the *locus in quo* of individual development and the unit of social expectation: "marriage", whether celebrated or uncelebrated, socially contracted or uncontracted, or simply conspicuous by its absence, remains at the centre of "family life". I think it does so because the idea of a couple coming together to produce a child is central in our psychic life, whether we aspire to it, object to it, realize we are produced by it, deny it, relish it, or hate it. Our imaginative literature, as well as an enormous quantity of professional writing, testifies to the family being seen as the source of our satisfactions and dissatisfactions—the origins of our strength and security or the hotbed of our neuroses.

It is therefore reassuring to find a book like this, in which the complexities of the subject are taken at depth in a serious and sustained way. The authors of the various papers focus on what may seem to some to be esoteric and complicated psychoanalytic concepts. They do so because these concepts explain much of the suffering and destructiveness that they see as marital therapists. Two of the concepts at the centre of this book—the *Oedipus situation* and *projective identification*—are at the heart of marriage and are probably more obvious in the relationship of couples and parents with children than anywhere else.

It might surprise some (though I still find it surprising that it *does* surprise many intelligent, educated people) that the vicissitudes of marriage begin in infancy. However, that, at least, is common ground in all the different psychoanalytic schools of thought. Infancy's vicissitudes (here mainly conceptualized in terms of Bion's theory of containment) are subsequently organized by the configuration of relationships that has acquired and retained the name of "the Oedipus situation". As children, we relate to our two parents both as separate individuals and together as a couple. Inherent in most of the thinking of this book is a theory of pre-conception: to adapt a phrase from Winnicott about the "breast" and apply it to "the couple": *before there was a couple, there was an idea of "a couple"*. In our adventures within the Oedipus situation, at different times we occupy different positions: mother's lover and father's rival, and father's lover and mother's rival, for both sexes, was the substance of Freud's Oedipus complex. He added as a precursor the "primal scene", where the child was the witness in fact or imagination of the parental sexual relationship. Klein grafted this onto her account of the Oedipus situation, in order to complete it. This is not the end of the story, though, as the cases in this book testify. We move through the different places in the "Oedipus situation" open to us in our everyday lives and nowhere more than in marriage. Our freedom to move psychically within this triangle has a great deal to do with our flexibility in intimate relationships and in our thinking itself.

The other phenomenon culled from psychoanalysis that is studied as a factor in intimate relationships is *projective identifi-*

cation. This is a term that, partly for historical and partly for clinical reasons, is conceptually confusing. Fortunately for the reader, a clear account is offered in the book of the development and usage of projective identification as a concept, together with excellent examples of it in action. It always co-exists with introjective identification, and both of them are part of normal life; they are crucial to development, and both are a possible source of maldevelopment. Without projective identification, there is no empathy; with *excessive* projective identification, there is a loss of separateness and accurate identity of self or other. As the book amply illustrates, no human field of activity compares with marriage in providing an opportunity for the use of projective identification, whether usefully in empathic understanding, or pathologically to disencumber the self of unwanted attributes by foisting them on the other, or to lay claim by identification to the desirable qualities of the other. Thus, within these papers and the interview with Donald Meltzer, there is ample opportunity for the reader to form an impression of the phenomena described under the title "projective identification" and the variety of theories about it.

For the marital therapist, psychoanalysis offers a source of theories which facilitates work with couples; for the psychoanalyst, the sort of work being done in the Tavistock Marital Studies Institute is a good example of applied analysis. This book celebrates the fruitfulness of the union of the two.

INTRUSIVENESS
AND INTIMACY
IN THE COUPLE

Introduction

Stanley Ruszczynski & James Fisher

We chose the theme of "intrusiveness and intimacy" as the title for this book in order to focus on a central dilemma in the life of a couple. We could say that the wish for intimacy defines a couple relationship. Sometimes the wish to be close, to be intimate, is associated with a concern for the other. This capacity for concern is a developmental achievement linked, in the language of Melanie Klein, with the depressive position. Sometimes, however, the apparent intimacy is an expression of an intrusive determination to control the other. At heart such an intrusiveness consists in treating the other as an extension of the self—what might be thought of as "narcissistic" relating. In other words, it is an "intimacy" of projective identification, an intimacy, we suggest, that is delusional insofar as it denies separateness.

This does not mean, however, that all relating in which there is a state of fluid ego boundaries is narcissistic. It could be said, for example, that in the early mother–infant relationship, when the infant has an especially undefined sense of the boundary of the self, there can be a benign sense of oneness rather than an intrusive denial of separateness. The chapters in this book do not share the same view on this and related questions but,

1

rather, focus the discussion of intrusiveness and intimacy in different ways, exploring and illustrating related aspects of this theme. While differences exist, one thing that is shared is the centrality of the notion of projective identification in our thinking. We thought it useful, therefore, by way of an introduction to review some of the history of this important concept.

Ever since Melanie Klein described the paranoid–schizoid position and outlined the schizoid processes of splitting and projection that characterize the paranoid–schizoid state of mind and type of object relating, projective identification has had an increasingly central place in psychoanalytic theory and practice (Klein, 1946). By 1952, when she gave more emphasis to the concept of "projective identification" in a revision of her 1946 paper (Klein, 1952b), some of her colleagues were already making clinical use of these new ideas (Rosenfeld, 1947, 1950; Segal, 1950).

These ideas, especially the notion of projective identification, have also had a central role in the psychoanalytic understanding of the couple relationship and in psychoanalytic psychotherapy with couples from the earliest days in the work of the Family Discussion Bureau (the earlier name of what is now the Tavistock Marital Studies Institute) and in the Marital Unit of the Tavistock Clinic (Dicks, 1967; Pincus, 1960; Ruszczynski, 1993). Indeed, it is not possible to understand this approach to the couple relationship without an appreciation of the centrality of projective identification. It is one of the aims of this present volume to show how this notion is used—and critically assessed—by psychotherapists working in the Tavistock Marital Studies Institute as well as by others interested in the couple relationship.

In her papers, Klein described the defensive projection into an object of split-off parts of the self and internal objects. This creates a particular type of object relationship whereby the object becomes equated with these split-off parts. In her paper "On Identification", she explores this process in the fictional story of a man named Fabian in the novel *If I Were You* by Julian Green (Klein, 1955). She describes the changes brought about in the identity of the subject as a result of the subject's projection of parts of the self into the object and in phantasy identifying with aspects of the object as if these were part of the identity of the object.

These projective and introjective processes operate in inter-action with each other from the beginning of life and build up the internal world of the self. Though the paranoid–schizoid anxie-ties, defences, and types of object relations are characteristic of the earliest stages of life—followed by those of the depressive position—it is important not to consider these to be stages or phases in development. It is more accurate to think of a constant and dynamic fluctuation, throughout life, between the paranoid–schizoid position and the depressive position.

Though the concept of projective identification was first de-scribed by Melanie Klein, it is those who followed her who have discussed it extensively and have developed its understanding. Spillius cites Segal in noting that Klein herself "was apparently always somewhat doubtful about its value because of the ease with which it could be misused" (Spillius, 1994, p. 339). Klein used the term to refer to an unconscious phantasy that influ-ences the way in which the subject experiences the object. Parts of the self and internal objects are projected into the object, which is then related to as if possessing the projected attributes. Klein emphasized the aggressive element in the phantasy in that it is a phantasy of forcing something into the other in order to control the other.

Perhaps the most revolutionary development in the under-standing of the idea of projective identification is found in the work of Bion, who, through his clinical experience with psy-chotic patients, came to talk about it as if it included the capacity to induce the other to feel what is being projected. In that sense the concept may be considered to refer to a primitive form of communication.

It is interesting that in the *Brazilian Lectures*, when Bion was asked about his understanding of projective identification, he responded with the "orthodox" Kleinian view that it was an om-nipotent *phantasy*—that is, an unconscious phantasy in which unwanted aspects of the self, for example unpleasant, unwanted feelings, are omnipotently split off and projected into the other. He went on to add:

> I am not sure from the practice of analysis, that it is *only* an omnipotent phantasy, that is, something that the patient *cannot* in fact *do*. I am sure that is how the theory should be used—the *correct* way of using the *correct* theory. But I do

not think that the correct theory and the correct formulation happen in the consulting-room. I have felt, and some of my colleagues likewise, that when the patient appears to be engaged on a projective identification it *can* make me feel persecuted, as if the patient can in fact split off certain nasty feelings and shove them into me so that I actually have feelings of persecution or anxiety. If this is correct it is still possible to keep the theory of an omnipotent phantasy, but at the same time we might consider whether there is or not some other theory which would explain what the patient does to the analyst which makes the analyst feel like that, or what is the matter with the analyst who feels as he does. *The trouble with theories is that they so soon make themselves out of date.* [Bion, 1990, p. 68; italics added]

Spillius writes: "It is perhaps unfortunate that Bion did not develop a special term for the behaviour the individual uses to induce another person to behave in accordance with his or her phantasies . . ." (Spillius, 1994, p. 340). Although she argues for retaining a broad understanding of the concept, she does suggest distinguishing between "projective identification as a phantasy, and the behaviour unconsciously used by the individual to get the object to behave in accordance with the phantasy" (Spillius, 1994, p. 340).

With other Kleinian thinkers, Feldman is clear that this "enactment" aspect of projective identification is of central importance. In his paper on "Projective Identification in Phantasy and Enactment" (Feldman, 1994) he credits Betty Joseph's important series of papers for making clear how the patient draws the analyst into forms of enactment that function as complex defensive organizations. It is also important to note Sandler's critique of the Kleinian and post-Kleinian description of this process. He suggests the terms "actualization" and "role responsiveness" to describe the way the person using projective identification gets the object to behave in a way that satisfies the unconscious wishes (Sandler, 1976, 1987). This view finds some resonance with Colman's approach in chapter four.

In part one of this book, in chapter one, "Narcissistic Object Relating", Stanley Ruszczynski describes the development of these schizoid processes and focuses in particular on the *narcissistic* nature of the object relationships that are more under the influence of the processes of projection, introjection, and projective identification of the paranoid–schizoid position. He suggests that narcissism and narcissistic object relations should not be considered to delineate only more disturbed ways of relating but are as likely to inform aspects of all relationships, at different times, to a greater or lesser degree. As all the other authors in the book, he uses clinical illustrations to show how internal object relations are enacted in the nature of interpersonal relationships.

He also argues strongly that it is important to see that projective identification refers to a mental mechanism that is *both* intrusive *and* a form of communication. He follows the view of Betty Joseph that it is often difficult to determine whether projective identification is "aimed" at communicating a state of mind non-verbally or whether it is aimed at entering and controlling the object. He shows in clinical examples how the therapist's capacity to experience and think about projections, even extremely intrusive ones, makes it possible for them to be experienced as a form of communication.

In chapter two, "The Projective Gridlock: A Form of Projective Identification in Couple Relationships", Mary Morgan draws on her psychoanalytic work with couples, giving detailed clinical illustrations from therapy with a particular type of couple relationship. She shows how some couples become trapped in what she evocatively calls a "projective gridlock"—a pathological organization in which projective processes are used rigidly and inflexibly for defensive purposes. She makes use of Rosenfeld's developments of Klein's ideas (e.g. Rosenfeld, 1965, 1987) in which he emphasizes the more defensive and destructive aspects of projection, identification, and projective identification.

Morgan stresses that a shared terror about psychic survival creates a particular type of couple relationship encased in a fixed matrix of projective processes, which inhibits any meaningful interaction between the partners or between the couple and the therapist(s) other than a maintenance of a deadly defensive equilibrium. She carefully explores the difficult technical issues for psychotherapists in therapy with couples locked in this almost impervious pathological organization.

One of the critical points of the healthy development of the personality is the emergence of an internal parental couple

(Britton, 1989). In the course of infantile development, as understood by Klein and others, there is a constant interaction of projective and introjective processes building up an internal world for the infant, most importantly the relationship of an internal parental couple. It is built up by the complex interaction between the infant's experiences of the external parental figures and forces operating from within the infant which shape and colour its experiences. In the paranoid–schizoid position there can be an attack on the internal parental couple, a particular kind of splitting that O'Shaughnessy (1989) describes as the "fracturing" of the parental couple. She also refers to the result of this "fracturing" as a "remnant couple" (O'Shaughnessy, 1993).

In chapter three, "From the Internal Parental Couple to the Marital Relationship", Giovanna Di Ceglie uses detailed descriptions of psychoanalytic work with individual patients to demonstrate conflicting attitudes towards the internal parental couple. The inability to tolerate the feelings towards this essential couple—feelings such as envy, jealousy, and the wish to control—leads to a dilemma she describes as "much ado about nothing". In her clinical analysis she illustrates three different types of images of the internal parental couple. These parental couples are split, or attacked by an envious ("Don John") part of the self, or virtually non-existent because they are attacked as soon as they appear. She demonstrates with great clarity how these influence the nature of the transference–countertransference relationship and infers how these also affect the types of interpersonal relationships these individuals create in their lives.

Di Ceglie's chapter reminds us of the central Oedipal struggle of ambivalence in relation to the parental couple, which is both looked to in love and attacked in hatred. If the reality of the parental relationship cannot be tolerated by the infant and hence cannot lead towards the development of the depressive position (Britton, 1992b), it may come to create a terrifying internal object relationship based on the more primitive and part-object relationships of the paranoid-schizoid position. Di Ceglie shows how internal object relations based on such persecutory anxieties and the attendant defences militate against any real possibilities of establishing anything other than the most disturbed and fragmented interpersonal relationships.

In chapter four, "Gesture and Recognition: An Alternative Model to Projective Identification as a Basis for Couple Relationships", Warren Colman takes up the discussion about projective identification and argues for clarification of the different processes to which the term refers. He discusses his view that the concept is not sufficient for understanding the mutuality characteristic of adult couple relationships. Colman acknowledges the view that projective identification, based on mutual anxieties and defences, may influence substantially a couple's initial attraction to each other, as well as the nature of their subsequent relationship (Ruszczynski, 1992). However, he suggests a different paradigm.

After stating his preference for retaining the term "projective identification" for defensive processes subsequent to early communications between infant and mother, Colman turns to Winnicott's notion of the infant's "gesture" and the mother's "response", based on her maternal preoccupation, to outline early processes of communication. He emphasizes the notion of an interactional field between subject and object and goes on to differentiate between projective identification and identification, stating that mutual identification creates the couple's sense of "us". In this "mutual identification" each partner has the capacity to retain a sense of identity *and* at the same time identify with the other. Such a capacity demands a "fluid" ego boundary that is itself a sign of mental health and internal security.

In chapter five, "Identity and Intimacy in the Couple: Three Kinds of Identification", James Fisher also focuses on identificatory processes in a way that complements Colman's analysis. He seeks to put projective identification in the context of other kinds of identifications, each with a corresponding sense of identity. Turning to the writings of Meltzer, and in particular his recently published long essay, "Sincerity" (Meltzer, 1971/1994), Fisher delineates three types of intimacy based on three different types of identification. Using detailed clinical material, he illustrates the three broadly different types of identification or sense of identity—infantile, narcissistic, and introjective. He goes on to suggest three different types of intimacy—infantile, delusional, and mature—which are linked with the three kinds of sense-of-identity.

Fisher stresses the importance of the description of the state of mind of the subject in each of these identificatory processes. Thus the state of mind of someone who is in projective identification with an object is something that can be observed and experienced in the clinical encounter when the kinds of details of unconscious phantasies that emerge in dreams are not available. This descriptive approach to infantile, narcissistic, and introjective states of mind is particularly relevant in psychoanalytic therapy with couples, where dreams are brought less frequently than in individual therapy.

Part two of the book consists of a discussion between Donald Meltzer and James Fisher, prefaced by a brief introduction to the discussion. Meltzer is a major contributor to post-Kleinian developments in psychoanalysis, and in chapter six he discusses a number of his areas of interest. Although the topics are wide-ranging, Fisher focuses much of their discussion on theoretical and clinical issues relating to the nature of the intimate couple relationship and psychoanalytic work with couples.

Although Meltzer does not work clinically with couples—indeed, perhaps precisely because he does not work with couples—he offers some provocative thoughts for those who do. He does occasionally supervise psychoanalytic therapy with couples and thus has some experience of this way of working. For example, in relationship to the debate within the field of psychoanalytic couple psychotherapy over whether the clinical focus of interest should be on the relationship between the couple—their "transference" to each other—or on the nature of their transference(s) to the marital therapist(s), Meltzer makes clear his agreement with the view that transference is understood to emerge in the *totality* of the analytic situation. Thus *all* the dynamics in the consulting-room between *all* those present are available for observation and interpretation.

Meltzer also expresses his reservations about the use of co-therapists in joint work with a couple. Acknowledging the already rich but highly complex transference–countertransference field created by there being a couple in the consulting-room with just one therapist, he wonders what advantages there are in further complicating the encounter by the presence of a second therapist.

These are only two of the many technical and theoretical issues that arise in this exploration of Meltzer's thinking and clinical experience, which include topics such as projective identification with internal objects, the nature of interpretation, the characteristics of the claustrum, and the nature of "falling in love", among many others. It can be read by those acquainted with Meltzer's writings as an opportunity to listen to him talk about familiar themes in an informal setting. For those unacquainted with his work, it can be read as an introduction to some ideas that readers may want to pursue, although at times the ebb and flow of spontaneous discussion means that many topics are mentioned but not elaborated.

A reading of this book will no doubt be a stimulus both to those working in psychotherapy with couples and to other psychotherapists, analysts, or counsellors who may find ideas that further their understanding of the psychoanalytic process with couples as well as with individuals. We believe that the book as a whole will be seen as an illustration for all clinicians of the extraordinarily rich field offered by clinical work with couples for further research into the primitive processes and object relations illuminated by psychoanalysis.

PART ONE

CHAPTER ONE

Narcissistic object relating

Stanley Ruszczynski

In this chapter I consider the concept of projective identification primarily by reviewing narcissism and narcissistic object relating in the clinical situation. I discuss couple relationships that present with narcissistic features, often considered to be a particularly difficult constellation of intrapsychic and interpersonal object relations.

I also put forward the thesis that projective identification refers to a mental mechanism that is *both* intrusive *and* a form of communication. In proposing this view, I follow that put forward by Betty Joseph, amongst others, who writes that, "it is frequently difficult to clarify whether, at any given moment, projective identification is primarily aimed at communicating a state of mind that cannot be verbalized by the patient or whether it is aimed more at entering and controlling or attacking the analyst, or whether all these elements are active and need consideration" (Joseph, 1987, p. 175). She arrives at a view that, providing we can tune into it, "projective identification is, by its very nature, a kind of communication, *even in cases where this is not its aim or its intention*" (p. 170; italics added).

Initial presentation
and clinical atmosphere

The type of couples whom I might eventually describe as narcissistic often approach the psychotherapist not with a specific problem or symptom, but, more usually, with a pervasive sense of mutual frustration, antagonism, and deep disappointment. I am often puzzled both as to what has held them together for the years of their relationship and why they are seeking treatment at this particular time. There seems to have been no sense of mutual regard or affection, but more a distancing coldness, aloofness, or self-sufficiency. Alternatively, there may be a confused togetherness, equally unsatisfactory, with no real sense of individuality or healthy separateness. Both report being dominated by the needs of the other; alternatively, each complains of being ignored by the other. Rather than concern, there is more often blame, accusation, and denigration. Alternatively, there may be an unconscious despair or terror at the thought of something going wrong between them. Sometimes this terror becomes conscious. Many such couples oscillate unpredictably between the aloofness and the confused togetherness.

Professionally, socially, and materially some of these couples may be "successful", with the frustration and sense of failure residing in the marital relationship. For others, the agitated disappointment is pervasive across all aspects of their lives. I have often been struck by the extremes of their interaction, demonstrated, for example, by a fluid combination of fixedness and volatility.

I am reminded of a couple I recently saw for a consultation. They had been together for over 30 years, having first known each other as childhood sweethearts. They had married, brought up four, now adult, children, and both had been professionally successful. They described what sounded like a very staid, lifeless, but stable relationship, based largely, it emerged, on unconscious mutual denial and sacrifice. Four weeks prior to the consultation, the wife suddenly announced that she could no longer stay in the marriage. Her husband agreed that he, too, had had enough, and within ten days the couple had amicably agreed to separate and were now living apart.

The shock at the precipitate way in which they had acted was felt, it seemed, only by me. I eventually wondered whether once the deadly status quo of their marriage had been broken, the only way of dealing with a now terrifying threat to their psychic equilibrium was to establish a new equilibrium, at any cost. The "agreed" separation, achieved so dramatically and precipitately, was the new equilibrium. It seems as if this couple are dominated by a psychic organization that requires agreement as the primary aspect of their relationship. Differentiation, ambivalence, or conflict appear to be totally unmanageable. By a process of mutual projective identification with an idealized internal image of relationships this couple seemed to create object relationships that sustained their sense of equilibrium but were unreal and destructive in their outcome. (See Meltzer's comments on what he calls "doll's-house" marriages in chapter six.)

In the consulting-room with such couples, I find myself unable to think about or address them as a couple. I am more likely to get caught up with one of them. In clinical discussion with colleagues, I also find that one or the other of the partners gets lost, the discussion focusing on just one of them.

There will often be no real curiosity about the other partner, or about me, but a sense of controlling or getting inside the other may emerge. Boundaries become confused or obscure: what belongs to the self and what belongs to the other becomes difficult to differentiate, with positive or negative aspects of the other becoming identified with and even idealized. Because of this distribution of various aspects of the self and other, through the processes of splitting and projective and introjective identification, such relationships can be very unstable if not rigidly maintained. If the mutual control and fixedness, via these schizoid mechanisms, does not take place, psychic equilibrium and even psychic survival is felt to be under threat.

With the couple mentioned above, for example, they rapidly re-established a sense of equilibrium, through mutual projective identification, by agreeing that they should separate. *What was paramount was that they should be in agreement.* Any conflict, ambivalence, sense of loss, or uncertainty was completely absent from their thinking both during their marriage and now in their separation.

It is often difficult with such couples to retain a capacity for appropriate separateness: I find myself caught up in some way, or controlled, or feeling very disturbed by my relationship with them. My comments or interpretations are often ignored, devalued, or attacked. Alternatively, interpretations will be hijacked and repeated later, often in a distorted way, which perverts what had been said, or I might find myself becoming the object of their idealization, sometimes even being seduced by it. My therapeutic stance and work is frequently undermined, challenged, or openly attacked.

Object relating or not?

The poverty of such couple relationships and the attendant clinical problems raise the question as to whether marital psychotherapy is the most appropriate therapeutic intervention. One or both partners could be diagnostically described as narcissistic or borderline. Some clinicians might argue that such individuals are not capable of relating and that there is no relationship with which the marital psychotherapist might work. They could therefore suggest that such individuals are better treated in intensive individual psychotherapy. All of this may, of course, be true.

However, I would like to suggest that such couples *are* engaged in an object relationship, but one that is pathological in its structure. Paradoxically, such a relationship is unconsciously constructed and maintained *exactly* for the purpose of avoiding or defeating that which would be required and would emerge in a more healthy object relationship. The relationship has purpose and meaning for both partners, although it is purpose and meaning substantially influenced by the more primitive parts of the personality.

My view is that narcissistic object relating is rooted in the anxieties, defences, and types of object relations of the paranoid–schizoid position, within which projective identification plays a crucial role. Given that there is a constant dynamic movement, in all individuals and in all relationships, between the more primitive paranoid–schizoid position and the more mature depressive position, paranoid anxieties are likely to be evoked, at times, in all individuals and all couples, therefore arousing the defences and types of object relations of the paranoid–schizoid position. This being so, narcissistic object relating—based on the processes of splitting and projective identification—should be considered to be *not only* a discrete and highly pathological state, but as likely to emerge, more or less, as "pockets" of interaction in all intimate relationships. So how do we begin to understand narcissistic object relations?

Narcissistic object relations

The genesis of what came to be called "object relations theory" emerged in the course of Freud's discovery of the mechanism of transference. Through his clinical work he became acutely aware of the intensity of feelings experienced by the patient towards the therapist. This "discovery" of transference placed the investigation of the patient's relationships at the centre of psychoanalytic theory and practice.

Following his first realization of transference, Freud initiated a major theoretical and clinical leap when he became interested in the clinical and theoretical problems with homosexuality and paranoid psychosis. Though based on biographical and autobiographical information rather than direct clinical experience, Freud speculated that such individuals would not be able to make a transference. He understood this to be because of "[the] diversion of their interests from the external world—from people and things", which made them "inaccessible to the efforts of psychoanalysis" (Freud, 1914d, p. 74).

In a biographical study of Leonardo da Vinci, for example, Freud suggests that Leonardo's apprentices were treated as if they represented the artist as a young boy. In addition, Leonardo identified with his mother, and he related to the apprentice boys as he wished she had related to him. Freud uses this study to illustrate how the relationship to the real external object is repressed and the self is taken as a model in whose likeness objects of love are chosen (Freud, 1910c). This state of mind Freud came to call "narcissism".

Freud differentiated between anaclytic (or attachment) type of love—fundamentally, a love of the object that has nourished or protected—and a narcissistic type of love—a love of what the person himself is, was, or would like to be. In doing so, he postulated a primary narcissism in everyone, which, in some cases, dominates the nature of their object-choice.

By "*primary narcissism*", Freud meant a primitive *objectless* stage of infantile development, predating object relating, in which the infant takes its own body and ego as an object of its love. This notion of a primary objectless stage of development makes it possible to speak of individuals and couples who do not form object relations, leading to the view that such patients are not capable of developing a transference. Disagreeing with this view, I would simply like to suggest that perhaps the issue is more accurately the *nature* of the object relating rather than whether it takes place.

As a result of her clinical work with children, Klein arrived at a view different from Freud's. Rather than an objectless primary narcissism, she came to understand that *from the very begin-ning* the young infant has a rudimentary ego that engages in primitive object relations. The infant relates powerfully to the mother—or, more accurately, to those parts or functions of the mother that it is concerned with or in need of at any particular time. This unintegrated relating creates multiple identifications and, therefore, a multiplicity of internalized object relations. (In Klein's language, this should be referred to as "*part*-object rela-tions".) Though the infant may actually only be relating to a few people, it relates to them in their different aspects and with varying degrees and types of physical and emotional involve-ment. These are projected into the object and so colour the nature of the experiences and of the subsequently internalized object relations. As Klein puts it, "Every external experience is interwoven with . . . phantasies and . . . every phantasy contains elements of actual experience" (Klein, 1952a, p. 54). Early object relations are founded on this interplay of reality and phantasy.

Through this normal dynamic process of projection and introjection, an inner world is built up, made up of the multiplic-ity of now internalized object relations—good and bad, satisfying and frustrating.

This view, therefore, challenges Freud's idea that there is an initial objectless stage of development. Primitive relating to an object or a part object may, in fact, be complex and overwhelming in its emotional force. Equally, this view challenges the idea that there is no transference from patients functioning in these more primitive ways. It is more likely that the transference will be pre-verbal and, therefore, enacted, intense, precipitate, and changing.

I am reminded of another couple whom I recently saw for a consultation at the Institute.

When I opened my consulting-room door to let out the couple whom I was seeing before the consultation, the new couple were standing literally outside my door. I was given an enormous shock. Once I had regained my composure, I asked who they were and then told them that they were ten minutes early and invited them to return to the waiting-room from where I would call them at their appointment time.

During the next ten minutes, I experienced a most disturbing volatility of emotions. Firstly, I experienced an enormous sense of physical intrusion, almost of violation. My breathing became very shallow, and I felt persecuted by questions to myself. How had they got past the reception desk? How did they know which my room was? How long had they been standing outside my door? Had they overheard anything of the session with the couple who were with me? What did that couple make of their experience when I opened the door to let them out? What did I say in my shocked state? Did they notice my shock? Will I be able to work with them for the appointed assessment? And so on.

Alongside these perhaps understandable feelings of intrusion, I also found myself overwhelmed by a sense of urgency that I simply *had* to understand the meaning of this first brief encounter before I actually saw the couple for the consultation, and that without this understanding I would not be able to conduct the consultation. Though I knew that this was a totally omnipotent aspiration, I could not dislodge it from my mind.

In the course of the consultation, the wife told me how shocked she was at her husband's affair and his desire to leave the marriage. The couple shared a view that they had had a deeply romantic beginning to their relationship—they were from different countries and had for some years courted internationally—and the sudden affair and threatened break-up had intruded into and violated their relationship.

However, what I found more interesting in relation to my countertransference was when the wife talked with pride about being able to "read" people—particularly her husband. Suddenly to find that he was behaving in this totally unpredictable way terrified her, because it meant that she had not read him at all. What I eventually came to see was that she seemed almost more disturbed by this loss of her capacity to "read" her husband than by the possible loss of him.

The husband spoke with frustration and anger at being suffocated by his wife's constant claim that she understood him and knew what he wanted. He experienced this as her powerful attempts at controlling him. However, he was also made very anxious by the unpredictability of his own behaviour, which disturbed him. I suspect that though he protested at his wife's attempts to control him, he did gain some sense of psychic security and equilibrium from being read by or understood by his wife.

I use this illustration to demonstrate the enormous power and communicative potential of our experience with our patients. This brief vignette shows how in my earliest countertransference reaction, not only did I begin to become aware of some of the powerful dynamics operating within and between the couple, but also that a *number* of emotional experiences seem to take place alongside each other or even simultaneously.

Projective identification

To understand this multiplicity of experiences, Klein conceptualized schizoid mechanisms, paying particular attention to what she called projective identification (Klein, 1946, 1955), which she understood to be a primitive phantasy of splitting off and projecting parts of the self and internal objects and identifying with them as if located in another person. The concept has now been developed substantially, and for many writers it is central in the understanding of human interaction. Bion, for example, writes that, "the link between patient and analyst, or infant and breast, is the mechanism of projective identification" (Bion, 1959, p. 105), and he refers to the ways in which one person can induce another person to actually experience and/or behave in accord with the phantasies of the projective identification. Though there is debate as to whether the same term should be used only for the defensive evacuative process (Klein) or also for that which is understood to be at the basis of the means of communication and psychic containment (Bion), there is no doubt at all that it is a very useful concept (Spillius, 1988b, 1994).

The reason for its utility is that, for many writers and clinicians, the concept has been found to be *essential* in the understanding of both interpersonal and intrapsychic object relationships. The clinical study of narcissism and narcissistic object relating suggests that the apparent *dichotomy*, both theoretically and clinically, between the intrapsychic and the interpersonal, between the inner world and the outer world, can all too readily be overstated. Working psychoanalytically, and particularly with couples, we are constantly reminded, through our clinical experience, of the interpersonal externalization of intrapsychic images and phantasies.

I cannot, of course, review the literature on projective identification: it is enormous. What I will do is briefly remind you of what I consider to be a few major themes.

As first delineated by Klein, projective identification was understood to be an unconscious primitive defence mechanism whereby parts of the self and internal objects are split off and projected into an object, which is then felt to possess the projected attributes. This is an omnipotent phantasy; it involves the domination of the object and a denial of separateness and, therefore, a confusion of identity. It becomes clear therefore that if parts of the self are, in phantasy, split off and projected into an object and the object is then related to as if possessing these attributes, projective identification is a description of the process of *narcissistic identification*.

As Steiner puts it, "One of the consequences of projective identification is that the subject relates to the object not as a separate person with his own characteristics but as if he is relating to himself. He may ignore aspects of the object which do not fit the projection or he may control and force or persuade the object to enact the role required of him" (Steiner, 1993, p. 42).

Amongst their many contributions to psychoanalytic literature, Bion (1959) and Rosenfeld (1971), amongst others, substantially developed the concept of projective identification by stressing its communicative potential. They suggest that the person doing the projecting unconsciously acts in such a manner as to evoke, in the recipient of the projection, feelings appropriate to those being projected. Bion (1962b) further proposed the notion of container/contained, referring to capacities of the mother or psychotherapist to be receptive to, process, and give meaning to that being projected.

These developments show that projective identification is not simply an omnipotent phantasy, but, as Britton puts it, the patient, "takes steps to *give effect* to his phantasy . . . by the evocation or provocation of such an experience for the analyst, by . . . verbal and non-verbal behaviour . . . providing a primitive form of communication" (Britton, 1992a, p. 105; italics added).

A deeper understanding has developed, therefore, of the ways in which, for example, the patient in treatment, or a partner in an intimate adult relationship, unconsciously influences the therapist, or the partner, to become involved in and enact aspects of their internal object relations in the nature of their interaction.

In the psychotherapeutic relationship, for example, Segal (1977) speaks of the ways in which the patient "does things" to the therapist, and Sandler (1976) speaks of the patient "prodding" the therapist into a particular role in a way that affects the therapist. Betty Joseph describes with enormous conviction how patients "consciously and unconsciously structure the analytic relationship", drawing the therapist into the process, and so "make apparent the nature of [their] internal world" (Segal, 1989, p. 2). Brenman Pick summarizes this clinical understanding by stressing that: "In so far as we take in the experience of the patient, we cannot do so without also having an experience", adding that, "to suggest that we are not affected by [the patient] would represent not neutrality but falseness or imperviousness" (Brenman Pick, 1985, p. 46).

Spillius gathers together these theoretical and clinical developments and suggests that clinically we now have three ways of using the concept of projective identification: Klein's way, which stresses the defensive and evacuative function; Bion's way, which stresses the communicative function; and, closely related to Bion's way, Joseph's way, which stresses the pressure that is unconsciously put on the therapist to act out in a manner consistent with the patient's projections (Spillius, 1992, p. 63). Clearly, being receptive to and eventually becoming conscious of what is being projected creates a communicative connection between therapist and patient (and also, though much less consciously, between two partners in an intimate relationship).

In relation to the intimate couple relationship, falling in love may be considered to be one of the most striking examples of transference. The couple's mutual receptivity to, and acceptance of, each other's transference projections may be said to constitute their unconscious attraction and attachment to each other and, in that way, their knowledge of each other.

I would argue that this communicative potential both *depends on and is the product of the intrusiveness of the projective process.* As marital psychotherapists, we know that the projective process, which plays such a part in creating a marital fit, *relies on the mutual projective identification finding a place of resonance in the partner,* producing the collusion of mutual knowing that makes up the couple relationship. I am here using the word "knowing" in Bion's sense, referring not to intellectual knowledge, but to an experiential knowledge of another.

As psychotherapists, we also know how successfully patients can "get under our skin", intruding not only into our rooms, as with the consultation couple referred to earlier, but into our minds and into our somatic sense of our selves. Whether we

have the capacity, as psychotherapists, to process these communications is, of course, another matter.

Paranoid–schizoid and depressive positions

If all human interactions are to some degree constructed on the
basis of projective identification, with projected parts of the self
and internal objects influencing the image and nature of, and
therefore the relationship to, the other, we can conclude that *all
object relations are in part narcissistic.* The point at issue is the
degree, flexibility, and forcefulness of the projective identification. If the more primitive defences of splitting and projective
processes dominate the nature of the interaction, such object
relations will be more narcissistically structured. If there is less
splitting and if the projective system is more fluid, so allowing
for the projections to be withdrawn, then the nature of the
relationship will be based that much more on the reality of the
self and other.

As Klein went on to formulate her ideas of psychic development, she introduced the concepts of the paranoid–
schizoid and depressive positions. These are understood as
constellations of particular anxieties, defences, and types of
object relations, internal and external.

The paranoid–schizoid position includes persecutory and
paranoid anxieties, as well as the more primitive defences of
splitting, projective identification, denial, idealization, and denigration; therefore, object relationships are with part objects,
with the splitting and projection producing a denial of separateness and a confusion in ego boundaries.

The depressive position includes more depressive anxieties,
including concern and guilt and the feared loss of the object;
defences will be more manic and obsessional, with repression
taking the place of splitting; and object relations will tend to be
more on the basis of recognizing both the self and the other
person as a sufficiently whole and separate object, with all the
inevitable toleration of ambivalence that this requires.

Because these constellations of anxieties, defences, and
types of object relations describe states of mind and not develop-

mental stages, there is the possibility—indeed, the likelihood—of a fluid to-and-fro into and out of the two positions, according to the anxieties produced by the impact of the constant interaction between the internal and external worlds.

This conceptualization of the schizoid processes of splitting, projection, and projective and introjective identification, operating from the very beginning of life and likely to emerge at different times, clearly suggests a particular understanding of narcissism and narcissistic object relating. Klein wrote very little about narcissism. On one of the occasions when she did, she said:

> [A] typical feature of schizoid object-relations is their narcissistic nature which derives from the infantile introjective and projective processes. For . . . when the ego-ideal is projected into another person, this person becomes predominantly loved and admired because he contains the good part of the self. Similarly, the relation to another person on the basis of projecting bad parts of the self into him is of a narcissistic nature, because in this case as well the object strongly represents one part of the self. . . . When these parts have been projected excessively into another person, they can only be controlled by controlling the other person. [Klein, 1946, p. 13]

The paranoid–schizoid position or state of mental functioning may, therefore, be considered to be synonymous with narcissistic object relating. We can now, therefore, refer to narcissism as a state of mind produced by a withdrawal to an internalized good or bad object, not an objectless state. Likewise, narcissistic object relating can be seen as the state where the object is projectively identified with as possessing attributes of the self, which is what makes it attractive to the (narcissistic) subject.

Rosenfeld further refined a very important aspect of narcissism when he introduced the idea of "destructive narcissism" (Rosenfeld, 1971). This is a narcissistic withdrawal not to the good internalized object, but to the more destructive internal object. He describes how such an identification produces what he calls an "internal Mafia" or "saboteur", which acts to defeat the efforts of the more benign aspects of the self. We are familiar with this, in the negative therapeutic reaction from patients towards our therapeutic work: it can also be seen with couples in relation to each other, where the powerful destructive part of the self (or partner) tyrannizes the dependent needy part of the self (or partner) and prevents it (or the couple) from gaining access to good objects.

Awareness of the need for the object, in the paranoid-schizoid position, leads to feelings of envy of the object depended upon and hatred of the felt neediness. Segal writes of envy as the realization that the source of life and goodness lies outside the self. Narcissism could, therefore, be seen as a defence against envy (Segal, 1983).

A particular aspect of this destructive narcissism is where the projective identification is global: the *whole* self is felt to be projected into the object. This would be in the service of denying any separateness from the object. Rosenfeld referred to this as a symbiotic or parasitic type of object relationship (Rosenfeld, 1983), in which the subject appears to live inside his object. An omnipotent narcissistic phantasy held by the subject is that the object welcomes such a relationship, which then becomes idealized, and so the destructive nature of this degree of projective identification is denied. In chapter two, Mary Morgan takes up this particularly pathological projective identification and discusses the ways in which a "gridlock" of projections, as she calls it, traps the individual or the couple in a state of psychic sterility, a state that may be understood as being employed to defend against psychotic breakdown.

Meltzer, in his work on the notion of the claustrum (Meltzer, 1992), describes excessive projective identification into an internal object, again with the purpose of defending the self against psychosis. Meltzer, unlike Klein, is concerned to suggest that, as he sees it, projective identification needs to be understood primarily in relation to internal objects. (See chapter six.) With patients for whom projective identification is at the most extreme—producing psychic fragmentation and an absence of a sense of boundary between the self and the other—it is interesting to consider just how we would differentiate clinically between internal and external objects.

Clinical vignettes

JOHN AND JANE

I had been seeing John and Jane weekly for about six months. They reported having had an enormous fight when, a few days earlier, John had returned home unusually late, after midnight, and found Jane asleep. He became furious that she was not waiting to greet him, prepared to join him in whatever he may have wished for.

John's description of this event was extraordinarily denigratory of Jane, clearly taking absolutely no account of her needs or interests. By projective identification, she had become for John completely identified with a primitive idealized object, over whom he could assume complete domination and control. When he found his narcissistic phantasy challenged, with Jane, by being asleep, behaving separately from his projection, he became enraged and immediately turned to denigrating her.

Here is the switch from the idealized object to the denigrated frustrating object. In this state of mind, John had no capacity to see Jane's needs or her separateness. Sarcastically, he kept repeating that all that he had wanted was, ". . . a kiss, just a kiss, that's all"—suggesting the primitive orality of such a state of mind.

As I tried to explore this with the couple, I quickly found myself trapped in a dynamic that left me feeling that whatever I tried to say, I would be experienced as rejecting one and supporting the other, and that this could switch unpredictably. My interest in the force of John's reaction to his sleeping wife was experienced by him as threatening. The idea that I could have my own mind and be curious and different from him felt persecutory: I was then separate from him and no longer in his control.

In relation to Jane, I found myself equally taken over and used by her. She identified herself with my comments, took them for herself, and perverted them into attacks on John in her own sarcastic way. What it was not possible to explore with her on this occasion—though it was familiar to the three of us—was her capacity to withdraw narcissistically (represented on this occasion by her being asleep) and completely to ignore John's attempts to relate to her in more benign ways. For her, too, I could not be allowed to have an independent and separate mind but was incorporated and made use of for her own narcissistic purposes.

In my countertransference, therefore, I was having to contend with being either an idealized good object or a persecutory bad object, with being controlled, with not being allowed to have my independence or curiosity, and with being made use of, on this occasion, by the wife.

Paula Heimann writes that "The essential difference between infantile and mature object relations is that, whereas the adult conceives of the object as existing independently of himself, for the infant it always refers in some way to himself. It exists only by value of its function for the infant" (Heimann, 1952, p. 142).

This view also relates to the idealization and denigration of the paranoid–schizoid mode of functioning. With such patients, idealization and denigration can quickly change from one to the other. Alternatively, the idealization and denigration may get institutionalized, through projective identification, into particular aspects of the couple's life, so that one part is good whilst another part is felt to be deeply disappointing. For example, a couple I am currently working with describe a mutually loving sexual relationship, but they have come into marital psychotherapy because their relationship has all but broken down, with each viciously accusing the other of being "mad", thoughtless, non-communicative, and incapable of having a meaningful relationship.

A SECOND VIGNETTE: ROBERT AND JOAN

I have been seeing Robert and Joan twice weekly for just over a year. They requested psychotherapeutic help when they became increasingly aware of non-specific unease and discomfort, sometimes with explosive and bitter rows and an anxiety that their relationship would not survive. They are in the same profession and work in sister institutions.

As one session got underway, I noticed that Robert looked very drawn and agitated and was staring at Joan in an openly aggressive way. Joan immediately said that Robert had had a very good job offer from his senior colleague, which, if he were to accept, would be a significant career opportunity. He had been given a period of time in which to think it over. Since the offer, they had argued about it all week, and she felt attacked, angry, and distressed.

Quickly the couple re-engaged in the argument, and I could observe that as Joan—invited by Robert to do so—attempted to offer her thoughts, views, and encouragement, he kept insisting that she was totally uninterested and *simultaneously* accused her of trying to dictate what he ought to do. His violently oscillating perception was quite bizarre. Repeatedly wrong-footed and confused, Joan was driven to impotent, spluttering speechlessness, crushed by Robert's denigratory attacks.

I found myself struggling to trust my own experience of what I was observing. If I were to try to comment on it—though I do not know what I would have said—I would be perceived as speaking nonsense and attacked for trying to impose this nonsense-understanding on the couple. I had no choice other than to remain in a state of isolated confusion and anxiety, fearful in trusting my own perception and experience.

Robert had now become calmer. He turned to me and thoughtfully explained that he was in the final stages of constructing a work plan for himself whereby he would combine a number of activities, each of which he had sought out and secured for himself and which constituted more or less a full-time job. He was not clear how this compared to the offer made to him by his senior colleague, but he was tempted to pursue his own scheme.

What struck me was the dramatic contrast between Robert's mood and manner now and how he had been only moments earlier, and also how it compared to how I perceived Joan being left speechless, confused, and impotent. I was con-

scious of my very confused countertransference, in such
stark contrast to the clear, calm, and thoughtful way in
which Robert was now presenting himself. I had not been
capable of offering a useful comment, but Robert was now
apparently reflective and calm again. I had been rendered
impotent, and Robert had provided his own solution.

I came to see that Robert had a conflict aroused by the job
offer but seemed unaffected by it. Joan, as I saw her, and I,
however, were full of frightening confusions, doubts, and uncertainties. Robert retained his potency, whilst I was rendered
impotent, as was Joan.

I eventually understood that the job-offer had aroused
Robert's envy. The senior colleague had something substantial
to offer, and it was probably better than that which Robert had
"made for himself". Furthermore, if he took the job, he would
have to work under the senior colleague, rather than independently. This would arouse his fears about dependence and
commitment. These various anxieties were unbearable, and so,
through omnipotent projective identification, he evacuated his
confusion, doubts, and anxieties into his objects. He then identified himself with the more calm and thoughtful internal object.
Rather than engage with the ambivalent situation he was in—he
was both interested in the offer of the job and also interested in
pursuing his original plans—he split his internal experience and
got rid of the anxieties, leaving himself calm again.

This dynamic mirrors Robert's constant struggle with me
in the transference. Can I be allowed to be the senior
colleague–psychotherapist who may well have some interesting
psychotherapeutic work to offer Robert, or does he continue to
maintain his psychic equilibrium by using his own familiar
defences? Does he put himself into a position of dependence on
the therapy and me, or does he retain his narcissistic self-
reliance, identifying himself with an idealized internal object,
constructed as a result of evacuating the denigrated bad object,
including his doubts and uncertainties, and introjecting the
object's capacities for thought and reflection?

Robert's interaction with Joan can also be understood in a
similar way. However, she had a part to play in the state of
Robert's mind and in their interaction. Her own unconscious

envy of his job offer was projected into Robert, leaving him to manage an enormously envious reaction within himself. This aroused his narcissistic defences and the destructive attacks on her and on me.

Robert now turned to Joan and reminded her how helpful she had been on a previous occasion, when a similarly difficult career choice had to be made, and how instrumental she had been in assisting him.

This quite sudden reversal in his view of Joan into the now (near-)idealized object is another narcissistic feature. Rosenfeld writes:

> In my clinical observation of narcissistic patients the projection of undesirable qualities into the object plays an important part. The analyst is often pictured in dreams and fantasies as a lavatory or lap. This relationship implies that any disturbing feeling or sensation can immediately be evacuated into the object without any concern for it, the object being generally devalued. . . . the relation to the lavatory/mother in the analysis is frequently felt as ideal, because the patient feels relieved when everything unpleasant can be immediately discharged into the analyst. [Rosenfeld, 1964, pp. 171–172]

For the marital psychotherapist, Rosenfeld's last sentence could refer to the "lavatory function" of the marital partner, who may become idealized because the subject feels relieved that everything unpleasant can be successfully discharged into the partner.

Summary

I will end by giving a brief summary of how projective identification may be understood to influence the nature of object relations and particularly how narcissistic object relations are constructed (see Rosenfeld, 1964).

In narcissistic object-relating, omnipotence plays a central part. Through projective identification, the partner is treated as a possession of the subject or, alternatively, used as a container for the projections of the parts of the self needing to be disowned because they cause anxiety and pain. Identification is a central mechanism taking place through either projective or introjective identification. The two partners can become so identified that separateness is lost. Projective identification acts as if the subject colonizes the other or aspects of the other. Separateness between self and partner is defended against by mutual identificatory processes at the heart of narcissistic object relations. Awareness of separateness leads to feelings of dependence and, therefore, anxiety. Dependence implies a valuation of and a love for the other, and this, too, because of the inevitability of frustration, leads to anxiety, pain, and aggression. Dependence may stimulate envy of the good qualities of the object. Narcissistic object-relating obviates both the anxiety and aggression caused by frustration and awareness of envy.

Segal writes:

> The life instinct includes love of the self, but that love is not in opposition to a loving relationship to an object. Loving life means loving oneself and the life giving object. In narcissism, life giving relationships and healthy self love are equally attacked. [Segal, 1983, p. 275]

The tension between more benign and more narcissistic object relations, all constructs of the mechanisms of projective and introjective identification, will inevitably be enacted in the dynamics of a couple relationship. For the marital psychotherapist, this dynamic makes up the core of daily clinical practice, both as it is lived out between the couple and as it inevitably draws in the therapist. The capacity to discover meaning in the cauldron of clinical experience is the constant challenge offered to us by our patients.

CHAPTER TWO

The projective gridlock:
a form of projective identification
in couple relationships

Mary Morgan

In this chapter I introduce the term "projective gridlock" to
describe a particular kind of couple relationship in which
the couple have a problem feeling psychically separate
and different from each other, and hence create between
them a relationship in which they feel locked together in a
defensive collusion within which there is only very limited
growth. I explore the particular way projective identification
is used to create this kind of relationship, drawing on the
work of Klein and Rosenfeld. I further suggest that the creation of such a relationship develops from a different kind of
"unconscious choice of partner" than that usually understood by the notion of unconscious choice as developed
within the Tavistock Marital Studies Institute. I illustrate
these ideas with clinical material drawn from couples seen
for marital psychotherapy in both single and joint sessions.
Finally, I consider some technical issues.

Anxiety about separateness and difference

All couples in marital relationships have to struggle with the problem of intimacy versus separateness. They have to strive to find ways of being emotionally in touch with each other, establishing a satisfying sexual relationship and enjoying the feeling of being together as a pair, while at the same time holding on to a secure sense of being one's own person, fundamentally different from the other, with separate thoughts and feelings.

The couples I am concerned with in this chapter seem to have particular difficulties in this area. They have great anxieties about either allowing the other a separate psychic existence and/or in being themselves able to feel psychically separate in the relationship. They often describe a feeling of there being only one person in the relationship or a feeling of confusion between them about who thinks and feels what.

Some of these couples (perhaps the more healthy ones) come for help because, at least in one of the partners, there is an awareness that they are locked together in a way that restricts their capacity to be separate people and to be themselves and to develop. The wife of one couple wrote in her application form: "I have now come to a point—where I feel I want to be more independent—have my own ideas and thoughts. Up to now I have sort of let my life go to one side and taken on my husband's. I feel sometimes that I haven't been living my own life but his . . . I would like to feel my own identity. . . ."

Such a sense of confusion about ego boundaries does not mean that the individuals are psychotic in the sense that they cannot distinguish between internal and external reality. They do have the capacity at a cognitive level to see themselves and others as separate, but, at an emotional level, evidence that the other is *different* (and therefore separate) is experienced as persecutory. I believe this persecutory experience encourages a paranoid–schizoid state of mind (Klein, 1946, 1955) and leads to a solution from the repertoire of defences available in that position, essentially resorting to projective identification as a means of denying the difference.

I do not intend to explore much in this chapter why it is that evidence of the other is felt as so persecutory, though this is touched upon slightly in the later clinical material. In my own clinical experience I have found that this tendency towards anxiety in the face of separateness or difference links to two types of background. In the first place, where there has been sexual physical abuse, for example, the environment is experienced as unsafe or unreliable, and projective identification is often used to control objects in order to dissipate anxiety. In the second place, there is a wish to avoid frustration or an inability to tolerate envy, as described by Rosenfeld (1983) and Steiner (1993).

It could be said that these couples come together not to form a relationship, but to avoid a relationship, because relationships require that there are two separate people. When the therapy begins to work, they become psychically more separate, and the possibility of relationship emerges.

The use of projective identification in the projective gridlock (Klein and Rosenfeld)

In thinking about the problem these couples face, I have found it useful to explore the particular way in which projective identification operates in such relationships. Projective identification seems often to be used excessively and intrusively, with the aim, or result, that the other's separate psychic existence is denied. Instead, a comfortable sort of fusion or feeling of being trapped or imprisoned is created, which stultifies the relationship. Such couples could be said to be in a kind of "projective gridlock". This kind of excessive, intrusive, and essentially defensive form of projective identification is sometimes termed "pathological", in contrast to the more apparently "normal" form of projective identification, which has more fluidity, including the capacity to be receptive to the return of projected aspects of the self, as described by Bion in his model of container/contained (Bion, 1962a, 1962b).

In this model, Bion describes the experience the infant has when his mother is able to receive the projected feelings and, rather than react to them, can process them within her own mind so that she is able to make available to him a modified form of those feelings. The persecutory anxiety that forced the infant to project the feelings into his mother in the first place is then shown to be less destructive than had been phantasized, and the possibilities arise that these feelings can, after all, be managed.

There are two areas of Klein and Rosenfeld's thinking on projective identification that I wish to highlight. First, Klein's theory of projective identification is born out of the paranoid–schizoid position, in which persecutory anxieties predominate. Good and bad parts of the self are expelled and projected into external objects who become identified with the projected attributes. We know that projective identification has a range of motivations, including the hope for containment that Bion has described (and that is implicit in a developmental unconscious choice—see below). Klein emphasized, however, that in the paranoid–schizoid position, one of the main aims of projective identification is to get rid of unwanted experiences and aspects of the self, whether good or bad, and to control the object now identified with these split-off parts of the self.

In the course of normal development, the infant grows and develops a stronger ego, which then makes possible the recognition and taking back of projections. As a result of this process, both the individual and other objects are experienced as more whole and separate. It is in this area of development that the couples I am discussing have a problem.

The second point about Klein's theory to which I want to draw attention is that she saw the mechanism of projective identification as the means by which the infant, in its most primitive state, first establishes object relations, even though at the beginning this is "part-object relations" and the distinction between self and other is not clear. On several occasions she comments on the excessive use of projective identification, which exacerbates the confusion between self and object. For example, she describes how in excessive projective identification parts of the personality are felt to be lost to the ego and can result in an over-dependence on these external representatives of oneself. The object may then be felt to be loved as a representative of the self (Klein, 1946).

Elsewhere, she writes that some people in empathically projecting their feelings into another "go so far in this direction that they lose themselves entirely in others and become incapable of objective judgement". In the same way, "excessive introjection endangers the strength of the ego because it becomes completely dominated by the introjected object" (Klein, 1959, p. 8).

Rosenfeld, in his conceptualization of "narcissistic omnipotent object relations", describes the way in which, "the patient identifies [by projection or introjection] with the object, to the extent that he feels he is the object or the object is himself" (Rosenfeld, 1987, pp. 20–21). He saw this partly as a defence against recognition of the separateness of self and object and also as a protection against frustration and envy. (Some of these issues are discussed in chapters one and three).

Unconscious choice of partner

Projective identification, usually in a less extreme form, continues to link objects in adult life too. It plays a part in the process whereby couples unconsciously connect up to form a relationship. Rosenfeld observes that projective identification is the process involved in recognizing objects and identifying them, sometimes with the aim of making essential links with them (Rosenfeld, 1983). A similar theory underlies the concept of "unconscious choice" of partner (Pincus, 1960), developed over the years within the Tavistock Marital Studies Institute. This has been understood as the process whereby couples make a choice of partner based on the unconscious recognition in the other of disowned aspects of the self, with which there is, at some level, a wish to make closer contact, for developmental or defensive purposes, or both. For example, an active, competent, assertive man may choose a

partner who is depressed because he cannot bear to acknowledge these depressed feelings in himself, preferring to locate
them in his wife. At the same time, the woman may feel
anxious about being directly in touch with her more assertive
and competent aspects and prefer to locate these aspects in
her husband. The unconscious hope behind such a choice is
the opportunity for each partner to gradually own these split-
off parts of the self.

In the kind of relationship I am describing here, the process at work is different from that conceived of in the usual
notion of unconscious choice. In the more usual examples of
unconscious choice, the individuals concerned have developed, at an emotional level, an acceptance of difference, even
if they are still unable to integrate all aspects of themselves
and, therefore, continue to project these unacceptable parts
into others. In the relationships under discussion here, one
or both partners have made a narcissistic object choice and
are unable to tolerate separateness. Projective identification
is used less as a way of projecting aspects of the self into the
other, and more as a way of maintaining a particular state of
mind dominated by the phantasy of being one with, or residing inside, the object. They seek identification in a concrete
way, which is intrusive and psychically denies the existence
of the other or themselves.

It may be that a prerequisite for being able to make the
more usual kind of object choice is the experience of containment and the development of a sense of self. In the kind of
object choice described here, the experience of a containing
internal object is probably lacking, and therefore projective
identification is used defensively in an attempt either to control the object or to merge with it to create a state of
pre-separate bliss.

Clinical illustrations

At this point I should like to give some clinical material to
illustrate the way in which a projective gridlock is experienced in three areas of object relating: (1) intrapsychically;

(2) in the transference and countertransference relationship between the couple and the therapist; and (3) interpersonally between the couple.

All the material is taken from psychoanalytic work with couples, sometimes seen together, sometimes in parallel separate sessions.

A projective gridlock: intrapsychic manifestations

GEORGE

The first example is from a session with George, the husband in one couple in therapy; it illustrates the way in which projective identification is used intrapsychically, as a way of controlling and fusing with his objects (his father, his wife, and his therapist), and it also shows the beginnings of a shift towards seeing himself as more separate.

> In one session, George began by saying that one thing was troubling him a great deal. Sometimes when he looked at his face in the mirror he could see his father. When he looked at his body too—especially at his genitals and legs—he felt it was his father's. Even his handwriting was the same as his father's. He talked about having hated sharing a bedroom with his father as a child, and his disgust at his father's habit of peeing into a pot at night. He told me that Maria, his wife, had told him that her father had done the same thing, and that she also found it disgusting.

> I thought that George was describing the result of his strong projective identification with a dominating internal object—that is, his introjected father. The process I am describing is one in which the patient forcefully projects into the mind, personality, body, or some part of the object and then totally identifies with that object. This kind of projective identification has been described by Betty Joseph as the patient taking over and becoming identified with some aspect

of the analyst (Feldman & Spillius, 1989). In George's case, he had the concrete experience that he was trapped in his father's body or that his father was trapped in his, and he felt disgusted by the feelings this evoked.

> I put this to him and linked it to two things he had talked about earlier in the therapy. One was his saying that he felt he had the potential to be a rapist and that he felt he was either "just a penis" or that he should "cut it off". I considered this to be an identification with his father's attitude to women, who were seen either as whores or like the Virgin Mary. The other was that he had recently told me about having worn skirts in the past and the pleasurable feeling of being safe inside them, like a woman, and then afterwards feeling awful about it. I said I thought he was describing trying to get inside his objects in order to know and control them but then feeling trapped in a body that was not his.

> George said it was funny how pleased he had been as a child when he was told he was like his father, though this seemed a horror now. He then spoke of the murderous feelings he had had towards his father, his and his brothers' plans to murder him, and his own wishes to die, so as to escape from what felt like a prison.

I think that because of the nature of his projective identification with his introjected father, George wished to kill this internal object, inside which he felt imprisoned.

> George then described the experience he was having at that moment in the room. He said he was looking at the wooden sculpture/puzzle on the window-ledge behind me. [It is a male and a female figure and their two reliefs, which fit together; if fitted together, they become the original solid rectangle of wood, with the two figures indiscernible.*] He said he had looked at this many times and had been unable to look at the figures without seeing each as part of the other. When he had looked, he had identified with both the male and the female figure. Now, for the

---

*This is the sculpture shown on the cover of this book.

first time, he was seeing them as separate as well as knowing that they could be fitted together. He was very affected by this and said he felt this perception was fresh and new, as if there had been a skin over his eyes before. I said I thought he was glimpsing the possibility of being separate from his father, in whose body he had felt imprisoned. In addition, I suggested he was letting me know about his experience of feeling safe inside me (the skirt), but that he also felt he could be free from being trapped inside me (my sculpture/puzzle).

I think it was George's acute anxiety about his internal objects, which he felt to be unpredictable and dangerous, that forced him to try to get inside them and control them. This often resulted in his feeling trapped inside his objects and losing any sense of their difference from him. Someone who functions like this in his internal world is likely to function in a similar way with his external objects, particularly with his intimate sexual partner, who, in a sense, is reduced to the status of an internal object.

A projective gridlock:
manifestations in the transference
and countertransference

This piece of material from another session with the same patient, George, illustrates the way in which this kind of projective identification is experienced in the transference and countertransference. This example shows the subtle way in which George tried to control me, so that we could function as one.

George came into the room, smiling, saying it was a hot day, and he asked me, as he usually does, how I was, without, I think, particularly expecting an answer. Then, sitting forward in his chair, he took a tissue from the table and wiped the sweat from his face and neck. He said, "I feel you're different today: perhaps something has put you into a particular mood". He seemed anxious that I might not be in a good mood. I thought that at this moment in the transference he was relating to me as he had to his father, a man whom he often experienced as violent and unpredictable, and who created great anxiety in George. I then said I thought he was feeling that there was something a bit unpredictable about me today and that he wanted to reassure himself that this had to do with something other than what was happening between us. His anxiety dissipated at my use of the word "unpredictable", a word we had come to use often to describe his father. It seemed to free him—he became aware that he was experiencing me as his father and that I was not like his father. Subsequently the atmosphere became more relaxed between us, and he then went on to describe some of his father's early life.

He told me at length about his father being brought up in a rough area of a large city, where he was involved in gang warfare and was feared even as a child.

I found myself captivated by his material and listened attentively. I then realized that the tension between us at the beginning of the session was now totally gone and we were back in the position of feeling perfectly comfortable and in tune with one another. I wondered what had happened to that moment of discomfort earlier in the session when George had been uncertain of my mood and of what was happening in my mind.

I said to George that, faced with feeling that he could not gauge my mood and be closely in tune with me, he related a story in which he could count on me to empathize and to get us back in tune. George agreed with this and went on to describe the way he continually tried to get inside the mind of his objects. He talked about teaching in his spare time and spoke about his pupils, and he described how he often found himself struggling hard, on his own, to work out what they thought and felt, and he would then tell them. He was usually right, and then he felt that his anxiety was relieved and that he was in control. He thought he did this all the time, and that one of the reasons he succeeded socially was because he could gauge other people in this way.

George's experience of growing up was of the world as an unpredictable, violent, and persecutory place. He described in many different ways the phantasy of knowing and controlling his objects, in the way that Klein depicts the defensive use of projective identification in the paranoid–schizoid position. As I understood it, there was a massive projective identification into his mother's mind. His phantasy was that he would get into her mind and know what was happening there. There was, therefore, no difference between them, and everything was predictable and safe.

ANNA

Anna, the wife in another couple in therapy, repeatedly used the expression "you know what I mean"—a common-enough expression, but spoken in such a way that I felt it was unconsciously used as a way of denying our differences and making it difficult for me to assert my separateness. It became increasingly important to check with her what exactly she meant, despite a countertransference feeling that I already knew.

In one session, the last before a summer break, Anna started by telling me that her life had changed completely during the preceding week. She was then silent. After a minute or so, I said I wondered whether she thought I knew what had happened, and that was why she was silent. She said yes, she did think I knew, and then she continued to talk as if I did know. It was only until much later in the session that she told me she had begun a lesbian relationship, though she referred to this only in passing. It was as if, in her mind, I was there when it happened, or I *was* the woman with whom it had happened.

In the therapy with Anna I had the experience in the countertransference of a powerful pull towards oneness, a comfortable kind of fusion that was often hard to resist.

I think in this example there are elements of a kind of projective process at work that Rosenfeld described as "Nirvana-like experiences", which "involve a desire to live in a a state of pleasurable fusion with an object" (Rosenfeld, 1983, p. 263).

There were similarities and differences in my countertransference with George and Anna. With Anna there was generally a more benign sense of womb-like fusion. Similarly, there were times with George when I felt that I was so intuitively in touch with him that it was as if there were no differences in our thoughts. Both these experiences had a Nirvana-like quality. However, there were other times when being receptive to George felt like allowing a concrete and controlling intrusion into my mind.

In some couples these two ways of relating to the world—the seeking of a benign state of fusion on the one hand, and the need to control and intrude into the other, to come together in the "marital fit", on the other.

A projective gridlock: interpersonal manifestations

Now I would like to give some examples that illustrate the way in which this kind of projective identification is experienced interpersonally in the couple relationship.

TOM AND RACHEL

The wife in one couple, Rachel, reflected on how she and her husband Tom always did everything together: they studied together, shared the same interests, and operated as one. He would choose clothes for her, and when they went to parties Tom would speak for both of them. It never occurred to her that she might have a different point of view. She often felt that when they talked to each other, he would lose awareness of her presence, and it seemed that she, for her own unconscious reasons, had gone along with this. For a long time she was quite content in this situation, except that she had never enjoyed sex with Tom. Tom said that looking back, what had felt awful about having sex with Rachel was that he had worked out what she thought, felt, and wanted to such an extent that it was like having sex with himself; paradoxically, he had not really known what was going on for her at all.

In one session, Rachel spoke of being very troubled by her hatred of being penetrated by Tom in sexual intercourse. The way she described this led me to wonder whether intercourse with Tom felt in unconscious phantasy like a concrete intrusion not only into her body, but also into her mind, leaving her feeling invaded and completely robbed of herself. It was as if her psychic experience of the (physical) penetration felt like her own ego being threatened by the domination of the introjected object, as Klein described it and as quoted earlier.

Rachel's experience of growing up was one in which her difference, in a large family, could not be acknowledged. She felt forced into a particular mould—one that she could not easily fit. One of her most traumatic memories was of being forced to change from writing with her left hand to her right, which contributed to a feeling of unease about her body and confusion about whether her body was really hers.

In choosing Tom as a partner, Rachel unconsciously chose someone who fitted into her expectations, in that he would be in control and define her. Gradually, however, in the course of their relationship, she found that she needed to disentangle herself from a position in which she could not be herself. In a sense, her problem was the opposite of Tom's, in that she expected to be invaded and was vulnerable to this because of her earlier experience and insecurity about her sense of self. Although she had increasingly found this intrusive, I think nonetheless there was a way in which she sought this as a means of experiencing a kind of comfortable fusion, and she was very anxious about asserting her difference, which, to her, meant losing her sense of fusion.

Bob and Louise

Another couple, Bob and Louise, described a distressing cycle of closeness and distance. They usually managed to get close at the weekend, but they quickly came to feel merged into one. The words they used were that there was "no edge" between them, and it was as if they were an "amorphous blob". During the week they felt angry with each other, and Louise, in particular, had the experience that Bob was not there. She described a feeling of deadness when talking to Bob, because it was as if she already knew what he thought and felt. Bob recognized this experience, adding that it felt as if there was no spark between them. However, he said he did not want them to get to the point of being "completely separate". Such an idea made him anxious about them actually separating, and so he wanted them to be part of each other.

I think that in the experience of feeling like an "amorphous blob", Bob and Louise lost the sense of being in a relationship with another and then felt angry with the other for abandoning them.

Technical issues

Psychotherapists working with couples in a projective gridlock are prone to a transference and countertransference dynamic or enactment in which there are felt to be no differences, disagreements, or separateness. This heightens the technical problem of trying to differentiate between what is a useful or "correct" interpretation and what is simply part of the dynamic or enactment. There can be such a powerful pull to be fused or controlled that what seems to be a feeling of being in tune is in fact a pressure to be of the same mind, a confusion encouraged by the sometimes recurring experience that everything one says appears to be right. The therapist has to be in a separate position in order to make interpretations; as Winnicott says, it is only through being separate that we become objects that are available to be "used" (Winnicott, 1969). With these couples it can be hard to get into and maintain such a position.

This task of maintaining a separate position may be made all the more difficult because it touches a part of all of us that is susceptible to "Nirvana-like experiences", and because as therapists we seek to use our intuitive capacities and stay closely in touch with our patients.

I think the key to clinical work with such couples is in paying close attention to the countertransference, watching for a sense of all going too well, or for an uncomfortable level of intimacy, or a sense of intrusiveness and control, perhaps when the patient is quite literally picking up what we are feeling and thinking at any moment. Rosenfeld suggests that when such a "symbiotic phantasy" becomes projected into the psychoanalytic situation, "projective mechanisms . . . become part of the symbiotic processes rather than an ordinary process of projective identification, and it is not possible to concentrate on individual elements which have been projected into the analyst". It may then be important to interpret this phantasy as a whole rather than particular projections (Rosenfeld, 1983, p. 264).

Betty Joseph makes a similar point in discussing the importance of thinking of the transference as the "total situation". She describes the way in which a patient may hear interpretations and their meaning correctly, but instead of using the words and thoughts to *think* with uses them to unconsciously *act* with. The analyst is encouraged to partake in this activity, so there is a feeling of words being said, but the words are not really being communicated with. She highlights the importance of "focusing our attention on what is going on within the relationship, how . . . [the patient] . . . is using the analyst, alongside and beyond what he is saying" (Joseph, 1985 p. 157).

Conclusion

Some couples come to marital psychotherapy because they are in what I describe as a "projective gridlock". The container, if it exists, is very rigid and not really a container, in the sense that Bion describes, in which projections can be processed (Bion, 1962a, 1962b). To put it another way, the container is lacking what Bion has called "alpha function", and therefore thinking cannot occur. The "container", then, is more like the "claustrum" that Meltzer (1982, 1992) has described, entered through "intrusive identification". (For a discussion of marriage as a psychological container, see Colman, 1993).

Sometimes in the course of therapy, as the couple or the partner who feels most trapped gets fully in touch with how deadly this feels, it can seem that the only way to achieve psychic separation is by physical separation and ending the relationship. Separation is usually acutely painful, because it is experienced either concretely as a loss of part of the self, or, conversely, raises massive anxiety about the capacity to function independently. If, however, the couple are able to feel sufficiently contained by the relationship with the therapist/s, then it is possible to experiment with being psychically separate—a process that leads to really seeing the other, as if for the first time.

CHAPTER THREE

From the internal parental couple to the marital relationship

Giovanna Rita Di Ceglie

I t is not clear when the concept of the parental couple appears in the course of individual development or in the culture of a society. Psychoanalysis views the encounter with the "couple" as the most important psychic event. The cluster of emotions, phantasies, conflicts, and thought derived from that encounter is what is called the "Oedipus complex".

In the original myth, where people tend to act rather than think, there is a simultaneous encounter with and elimination of the couple: encounter with the father and patricide, encounter with the mother and incest.

In the various permutations of these actions in the theatre of the mind, the common denominator is the splitting of the parental couple and the denial of the generation gap. Psychoanalysis has discovered the connection between adulthood and infancy, between past and present, between the way we have emotionally

I would like to thank the patients who inspired this chapter. I would also like to thank Dr Domenico Di Ceglie and Dr Elizabeth Spillius for their helpful suggestions.

experienced the parents as a couple and the type of relationships we establish as adults.

Freud emphasized the sexual aspect of the Oedipus complex. Its conflicts, under the threats of castrations, were partially solved by identification with the parent of the same sex, the formation of the superego, and the establishment of the incest taboo towards the parent of the opposite sex. Further developments of Freudian theory and particularly object relations theory have made us familiar with a new language and a more complex way of looking at the Oedipus complex.

With Klein, it is not only the threat of castration that makes the child renounce the parents as sexual objects. It is also the active desire to love and the capacity to tolerate frustration that enables the child to let the parents have their creativity and to become creative himself or herself in due course.

Furthermore, in Kleinian thinking, the couple becomes an internal object, the development of which is part of an evolutionary process that is influenced, on the one hand, by the actual parents and, on the other, by complex vicissitudes of love and hate, guilt and reparative feelings, whose object is not just one parent or the other but, more specifically, the link between them.

Bion, in "Attacks on Linking", developed this particular aspect of Kleinian theory. With Bion, the link between the parents becomes part of a function that starts from the first link with the mother. When this link is made and is introjected, it enables the infant to entertain the idea that the parents share something special—that is, the idea that they are in a couple (Bion, 1959).

Britton, in his paper, "The Missing Link: Parental Sexuality in the Oedipus Complex", has developed this concept further. More precisely, he describes the triangular family situation, which provides the child with three different and coexistent emotional experiences: based on (1) his separate link with each of the parents; (2) on being the observer of and not participant in their relationship; and (3) being observed by them (Britton, 1989).

Shakespeare has splendidly represented this important aspect of development in "Much Ado About Nothing". The play develops around two pairs of lovers: Claudio and Hero, and Benedict and Beatrice. The play develops through the plots and machinations of Don Pedro, Prince of Aragon, and Don John, his bastard brother. The target of their activities is precisely the link between the lovers from the time of their first encounter.

It is evident from the start that Don Pedro plots the making of the couple. He wants to facilitate the encounter between the lovers, and he looks for allies for his plan:

If we can do this, Cupid is no longer an archer;
his glory shall be ours, for we are the only love-gods.

[Shakespeare, "Much Ado about Nothing", Act II, Scene 1]

Don John, his bastard brother, on the contrary, prepares plans that reveal his sadistic enjoyment in attacking and destroying the bond between the lovers, which is a source of feelings of exclusion, jealousy, and envy to him.

It is not difficult to see the defensive aspect of the two brothers' behaviour: Don John frees himself of intolerable feelings of envy and jealousy by making Claudio jealous and suspicious through the manipulation of reality. Don Pedro defends himself from the same feelings by thinking of himself as the maker of the couple. Don Pedro and Don John personify attitudes present in all of us. When these attitudes are not integrated, they create "much ado about nothing".

By attributing the constellation of negative feeling to the bastard brother, Shakespeare seems to have understood the relationship between the internal world of the adult and infantile experiences. The title "Much Ado About Nothing" adumbrates the complexity of feelings, the noise, and the interference generated by the existence of the couple, whose members had got together of their own accord.

The acceptance of this simple fact—a couple that gets together and makes babies—is not easy. In particular situations, tremendous feelings of exclusion, envy, and jealousy are made tolerable only through the phantasy of creating or destroying new couples that represent the original parental couple, which, in fact, could not be controlled.

The noise, the conflicts, the uproar of feelings generated by the parental couple is one of the most important objects of investigation in working with patients. Three different case studies show how this situation is reflected in the analyst–patient couple.

Mrs A

Mrs A started analysis in a state of severe depression. She felt completely worthless and the object of contempt, particularly from her mother. The world around her was felt to be squalid, and suicidal thoughts occupied her mind as her only solution. Details of her early years in Scotland appeared later in analysis. Her mother was described as a jolly and sociable woman involved in various activities as well as being a house-wife; the father, a headmaster, was described as a hard-working man, but rather weak and depressed. They were both described as very critical and intolerant of any disobedience by the patient, in contrast to their tolerance of the brother's mischief. He was only fifteen months younger.

Although Mrs A felt close to her father, she gave the impression of having felt very much apart. Locked in stubborn resentment, she grew up into a good little girl who was incapable of spontaneity. Successful in her studies, she completed her education abroad, where she became involved in many confused relationships, which produced two pregnancies, followed by abortions, in circumstances of isolation and total lack of support.

She later married a man who loved her. He had a grown-up son from a previous marriage and, according to my patient, wanted to have more children. Their marriage, however, was almost asexual, and she was worried that sooner or later her husband would leave her.

In the course of the analysis, it became clear that in her mind her parents did not feature as a couple, let alone a sexual one. They were two people who could not help one another, were needy of Mrs A, and were very critical and reproachful of her independence. On the other hand, the mother was experienced as having a privileged relationship with her brother, a relationship from which Mrs A felt completely excluded. It was this feeling of exclusion that seemed to unite her to the father, whom she saw as left out and excluded too.

Her marital relationship reflected both her internal version of her parents, living together without sex, and her version of the mother–child couple. She treated the husband like a child and demanded undivided attention from him as if she were a child. She dreaded the idea of children. They were experienced as intrusive and demanding and very much in rivalry with her to get her husband's attention, in the same way as she had experienced her brother.

The parental couple seemed completely replaced in her mind by the mother–child couple, and it was this couple with whom we had to deal first. In the analysis, she was extremely cooperative, bringing dreams and experiences, and I felt we made up a good mother–child couple. I soon realized, however, that a part of her could not be reached, as if, at another level, she had locked me in with a sibling, and I was felt to be totally inaccessible.

A dream she had where *she was separated from me by a thick screen* confirmed and substantiated my impressions. This secretive part of her came out in dramatic circumstances when she confessed her kleptomaniac activity at the time when she began to see how, by locking mother and child together, she had literally stopped herself from having a real relationship with either.

This was a very important step. For the first time in her life she took the risk of bring her "dirt", as she called it, to somebody—her analyst. The process that followed was extremely complex, this messy and secret part of her was so split off from the orderly, compliant one that had acquired a life of its own and was felt to be extremely menacing.

I will not discuss the analytic process that followed this confession. The point I want to make is that the stealing was closely associated with robbing her parents of the product of their sexuality so as to bypass the process of knowing about it. Stealing provided a solution, however precarious, to both problems: her parents' sexuality and her own. The absence of a sexual parental couple in her internal world, which was reflected in her marital relationship, seemed rooted in her early relationship with her mother, with whom the ordinary giving and taking was experienced as robbing and being robbed.

The birth of the brother, shortly after her weaning, estranged her from her mother, and she established with her father a marriage of mutual exclusion from mother and son. I would like to show now how this state of affairs manifested itself in the analytic relationship.

A week after returning from the summer holiday, she began the session by saying, in the voice of somebody who does not want to be noticed too much, that she had had a dream that she had not fully understood. The dream was *about a girl who slept with the mother, and a boy who slept with the father. The girl smelled terribly of urine. Her mother passed her clean linen to cover the mess up as quickly as possible.*

She then entered a state of total passivity, waiting for me to pass her my understanding.

When I want to underline here is that the request of the patient, which I understood without her making a contribution, expressed a desire to have my interpretations, but not as a result of the work done by two people together. In the analysis, a kind of robbery occurred, where she either robbed me or I robbed her. The understanding could not occur as a result of two people working together, but by a sort of parthenogenesis.

The dream is particularly interesting because it shows not only the split parental couple, but also the establishment of an internal object impervious to the infant's projections.

Miss B

Miss B revealed a different mental configuration of the internal couple in her analysis. She is an attractive American woman in her thirties and works as a lawyer. She felt emotionally blocked and anchored in her mind to a boyfriend with whom she had split up, in fact, ten years earlier. In her mind, however, the relationship had continued uninterrupted and was revived by his sporadic visits. He would appear from time to time, only to disappear again for months.

Sensitive and intelligent, Miss B knew that she was lucky to have had loving parents, but she felt deeply hurt by the very unsatisfactory relationship with her father, particularly by her lack of spontaneity and affection towards him. She had a younger sister, and it was not difficult to guess the tremendous rivalry behind her exaggerated declaration of love towards her.

Miss B had not been in therapy for long when she told me of her involvement with a man who was engaged to another woman. She told me that he was on holiday with his fiancé and had telephoned to tell her that he was thinking of her and that he had sent roses. She was outraged that he could do that but was totally preoccupied with the question "does he love me or not?"

I told her that her question was obscuring a reality she did not want fully to know about, namely the fact that the man in question loved two women at the same time and that she was giving him the impression that it suited her perfectly. In fact, she had expressed her outrage in the session and not with him on the telephone. Miss B was rather taken aback by what I had said, and it was possible, during the following sessions, to see how in her mind the engaged man was confused with her father, whom she could not really love, for fear of taking him away from her mother and sister.

She had manifested a great deal of concern for the fiancé. She realized that she was holding back her love and affection for her real father, while she was falling in love with men who, like her father, were engaged with other women. It is possible to see in this case how the patient repeated in her relationships the Oedipal situation that had been reached but not resolved. Something stopped her from resolving the experience of separateness as well as her feelings of exclusion and jealousy when the birth of her sister confronted her with her parent's creativity.

On the day of her 31st birthday, she was very depressed. She said that her 30th birthday had been fantastic, and, in contrast, she felt that this 31st birthday was not hers but somebody else's. Then, thinking of a job for which she had previously applied, she started to talk vehemently against the colleague who got it. She was very angry towards the interviewing panel because really they gave the job to such an ugly girl. I told her that her 31st birthday was felt as the birth of her sister, the number one added to three, the wonderful trio of her and her parents, and that her feelings towards her colleague who got the job really expressed her jealousy towards the new-born baby, who looked so ugly, and she could not understand why everybody kept looking at it in admiration.

She was very shocked by what I said, but she was able to bring memories of loss and isolation, which were linked to the way she felt that day. However, following the experience of becoming more and more aware of her internal world, she started to ruminate and to doubt the analytic work being done. I felt that my interpretations had made sense to her and that she had let them fertilize her mind, but they were then followed by an envious second thought, which would block any further understanding. It is interesting to note how again the transference reveals both the wish to be in a couple as well as the wish to destroy it. Similarly, in her life, her wish to have a creative relationship with a man is interfered with by the wish to split the couple.

With Miss B, the idea of the couple was quite developed, and the couple was felt to be creative but was attacked by a "Don John" part of her.

Mr C

With Mr C, the idea of the parental couple seemed to be totally non-existent, either because it had not been acquired or because it was destroyed as soon as it appeared.

Mr C revealed an internal world where he moved in a space without time, where the clock always told the same time, where there was no end or beginning, and he was continually surprised and persecuted by life, which passed by. A sentence he said epitomized his situation: "I am waiting for a bus which never arrives." In analysis, he was waiting for the illuminating interpretation that never arrived. He continuously tried to convince me of the cruelty of his father and the incompetence of his mother, which I had no reason to doubt, but the experience to be believed and listened to implied the existence of an "other" with a space between himself and the other, which he could not tolerate.

The disturbance seemed to have occurred very early in life in relation to his mother, and then a childhood of deprivation and violence had followed. His parents had beed divorced when he was in his late teens. They remarried, but for my patient nothing changed. He had only ever had one brief relationship, with another man, who then left him and married a woman. He lived at the margins of their relationship and described them in the same way he described his parents.

The problems in the analysis were considerable. There was a problem of surviving the session. The patient could not tolerate thinking, because it created a space in the osmotic relationship with the mother. This mother was more an environment than a person. Mrs C's need for an environment/mother bore similarities to the infant's need for a facilitating environment as described by Winnicott (1963) or for a marsupial space as described by Henri Rey (1979).

Bion, in his papers, "On Arrogance" (1958) and "Attacks on Linking" (1959), has advanced the hypothesis that these types of patients may have been deprived, as infants, of the use of projective identification and, as a consequence, they have introjected an obstructing object that forbids any contact based on that mechanism. This is consistent with the experience of extreme intrusion that one feels in working with these patients, as if intrusion is the patient's only way of dealing with an object that denies entry.

However, in his paper "The Missing Link: Parental Sexuality in the Oedipus Complex", Britton (1989) has furthered our understanding with his idea that such patients find the analyst's thinking intolerable because it is not differentiated from parental intercourse. This intercourse is felt by the patient to endanger the extremely precarious relationship with the mother and with life itself. The mother–child relationship is precarious because it is based on the continuous maintenance of splitting and projection of its badness into the father, who therefore has to be constantly kept out.

Britton's formulation would explain Mr C's unspoken belief that his well-being depends on the annihilation of the couple from his mind. Shakespeare's Don John puts this belief into words:

Any cross, any impediment is med'cinable to me.

[Shakespeare, "Much Ado about Nothing", Act II, Scene 2]

Conclusion

In this chapter I have presented some aspects of the work with three patients who have difficulties in establishing a satisfactory and creative relationship.

Mrs A, the first case, is married, but the marriage is deprived of sexuality. The second patient, Miss B, is capable of passionate relationships, but she becomes involved with men who are engaged in another relationship. The third patient, Mr C, is a single man whose only experience of a couple has been with another man.

I think that the cases of Mrs A and Miss B are similar inasmuch as I, in the analytic situation, was made to be a participant in a process of understanding, however difficult and disturbed it might have been at times. Their internal world was communicated to me either verbally or through projective identification. As a consequence, I was allowed to have a picture of their life and history and conflicts as they unfolded in the actual analytic situation. Projective and introjective mechanisms made up the analytic link.

With Mr C, what was communicated was the impossibility of communication, even as projective identification. The process of getting to know and be known was therefore blocked; what we had was a situation of impending threat of a paralysing nature if any enquiry were to be initiated.

In the case of Mrs A and Miss B, the analysis provided an opportunity for the employment of projective identification. I could identify the operation of a Don Pedro or of a Don John, felt to be in them or at times in me, which I could then interpret to the patient. In Mr C's case, there was an attempt to destroy any awareness of the existence of those forces vis-à-vis the couple, and I was often left, literally and not metaphorically, with much ado about nothing.

I have not referred here to the changes that took place during psychoanalytic treatment. Rather, I wanted to show three different levels of disturbance in the development of the internal parental couple, conceived as the result of an interaction between the experience of the real external parents and internal factors, in particular the wish for the parental couple to exist and the wish for it to be destroyed.

CHAPTER FOUR

Gesture and recognition: an alternative model to projective identification as a basis for couple relationships

Warren Colman

I n this chapter I propose a modification and limitation of the rather over-extended use of the term "projective identification". I suggest that some uses of the term may be better understood to refer to a state of fluid ego boundaries, which, in health, may promote a sense of mutual identification between individuals; this needs to be distinguished from the defensive uses of projective identification associated with splitting and denial. Mutual identification is based in early communication processes between mother and infant, which Winnicott (1960b) has described as the mother's response to her infant's gesture. These processes occur prior to the establishment of the infant's own sense of ego boundaries, which are required before projective identification can become a possibility.

My preference is to reserve the use of term "projective identification" for defensive processes subsequent to these early communications between mother and infant in which the mother's own fluid ego-boundaries—her "primary maternal preoccupation" (Winnicott, 1956) or "reverie" (Bion, 1962a)—enable her to respond appropriately to the infant's need to experience an illusion of oneness with her. However, since usage is a matter of shared custom rather than any one individual's definition, we shall probably all continue to think of this distinction as being between the positive, creative use of projective identification for the purposes of communication and its defensive use for the purposes of evacuation, control, and intrusion. My concern is less with the introduction of new terms than with clarifying the different processes to which these terms refer.

Projective identification and self-containment

Any discussion of projective identification is bound to be closely linked to the subject of narcissistic object relations. Since the object is identified with that part of the self which has been projected into it, projective identification denies the object its separate existence, its unique otherness. The concept implies, almost by definition, that the other is related to as if it were a part of the self—in other words, narcissistically (see chapter one).

This creates conceptual difficulties for the psychoanalytic theory of marital interaction, which regards projective identification as a central feature of partner choice and of the unconscious interaction between the couple (Ruszczynski, 1992). For it implies that all couples share this inability to be separate, or at any rate it leaves us without conceptual tools for understanding what does take place between couples who are able to acknowledge each other's separateness. The problem is expressed in this question: if partner choice is based on projective identification and the developmental aim of couple relationships involves the withdrawal of projections, what need would anyone have for a relationship if all projections could be withdrawn? There is something of a paradox here in that the aim of withdrawing projections is supposed to lead to deeper, stronger relationships, not to obviate the need for relationship at all.

It is this kind of conundrum that leads me to think that we may be using projective identification to describe too many different processes, resulting in problems that may have more to do with the conceptual map than with the experiential territory. I suggest that Bion's model of containment is essentially an account of early processes of communication in which, while there may be *identification* between mother and infant, *projection* does not yet play a part. Winnicott's image of the mother's response to her infant's gesture seems to me to refer to the same process but has the advantage of more clearly rooting the process in some recognizable form of social interaction—that is, an event taking place between two persons, which, as well as processing the infant's raw experience, also provides a model for what later social relationships will be like. As such, it provides a better image for understanding the analogous processes that take place within adult relationships.

Bion's distinction between realistic and "excessive" projective identification—or, as Meltzer has termed it, intrusive identification (Bion, 1962b; Meltzer et al., 1982)—takes us some distance along this path, enabling us to suggest that in more "healthy", "mature" relationships, projective identification is mainly restricted to the need to communicate and the wish to be contained by the other; it is only used as a means of evacuation or control at times of unusual distress. However, when applied to the symmetrical relationship of the adult couple, this still leaves open the problem of how the processing of projections might take place in a couple where, unlike the asymmetrical mother–infant couple or analyst–patient couple, there is a similar level of psychic functioning in both partners. At its worst, this can sometimes produce the tragic result that partners who choose each other on the basis of a shared understanding of some mutual deprivation or difficulty soon find that the other's very capacity to "know what it is like" renders them incapable of providing the different experience that is longed for. Their unusually high receptivity to each other's projections makes them simultaneously unable to process them. At this point, realistic projective identification may very easily tip over into intrusive identification as each partner tries more desperately to find containment from the other.

To some extent, my paper on "Marriage as a Psychological Container" attempted to address this problem by proposing that, in successful relationships, the process of containment as described by Bion becomes a function not of one individual or the other, but of the relationship itself (Colman, 1993). However, the conceptual problem remains in so far as projective identification is still regarded as the mechanism through which containment takes place.

It now seems to me that the level of containment in a relationship, and the means and extent for which projective identification is employed, is dependent on the level of self-containment of the partners. Here I am using containment quite literally to refer to a bounded space. Self-containment depends on the quality of the boundary that is felt to exist between the inside and the outside; the sense of ego-identity is a function of this boundary in that it defines the self as separate from others and possessed of one's own private internal world.

The nature of the couple relationship is a reflection of this internal situation of the partners. Since the process of partner choice and projective identification ensures that couples will create relationships that reflect the state of their internal world, it is usually the case that those who are most in need of containment are least likely to make relationships that provide it. The sense of gaps, leaks, and holes in their internal world—or, alternatively, of being trapped and walled in—is likely to be felt and enacted in the relationship created between the couple. The lack of a secure ego boundary creates a primary confusion about what is inside and what is outside. This may be exacerbated by projective identification but, in my view, is not originally caused by it.

Therapeutic intervention in these relationships provides the partners with a shared experience of an encounter with the internal world of an other who does not simply reflect their own internal situation. Interpretation challenges their mutual assumptions and therefore creates a boundary in itself. This encounter with difference may be as important a feature of an interpretation as its actual content. In foursome therapy (where two therapists work jointly with the couple), the co-therapist couple additionally provides an encounter with a *relationship* that does not simply reflect the couple's own relationship, albeit considerable work may need to be done in the countertransference to ensure that this is the case.

Clinical vignette

Before going into detail about how the bounded space of self-containment is—or is not—developed through the early pro-cesses of communication between mother and infant, I would like to root this discussion within couple interaction by giving a clinical illustration of a couple who presented severe difficulties with ego boundaries. This couple were seen by myself and a female co-therapist for a period of three years, almost entirely in joint foursome sessions. I shall select only those details that are relevant to my current purpose, focusing on a particular aspect of a session in which I was able to recognize and interpret the couple's boundary confusions; the description does not attempt to give an account of the actual nature of foursome therapy or the contributions made by my co-therapist.

ERIC AND CAROL

Eric and Carol were the sort of couple who frequently argued about the reality of events, with each one giving a totally different account of what took place between them and accus-ing the other of gross exaggeration, distortion, and downright lying. Their relationship was surrounded by an atmosphere of chaos and enormous anxiety about lack of money. Carol would frequently erupt into violent emotional storms while Eric tended to maintain a Micawber-like optimistic denial, oscillating between attempting to mop up Carol's emotions and absenting himself, particularly to the pub.

The session I wish to describe took place at the beginning of the third year of therapy. It began with Eric saying that he had some kind of virus cold-bug. He hoped we would not catch it from him. He began to talk about feeling depressed, but Carol immediately changed the subject. When the thera-pists pointed this out, she said she was worried that if Eric talked about his depression, she would also get depressed.

Eric went on to talk about intermittent bouts of extreme self-consciousness at work when he would suddenly feel inauthentic and worthless, as though he were not a valid person. He linked this to his preference for sitting with his back to the light so that his face cannot be seen—something that goes back to his schooldays, when other children would point out the severe eczema on his face. He felt as though he might give something away he did not want to.

I interpreted that he felt as though his inside might suddenly get outside, as though he were transparent, linking this to his shame about the public visibility of his private eczema, which made him feel literally as though he hadn't got a skin.

Eric said he thought Carol was more authentic because she always let her emotions out, but Carol said she was coming to realize that her emotional outbursts were really histrionic displays, which defended her against what she really felt. When she was a child, she had always been made to feel the bad one at home and had always needed to get out of the house—going off on her bike, for example. She now saw that her parents' worries about her getting into danger were valid—the other day one of their daughters had had a (minor) accident on her bicycle.

Eric said she always worried about what might happen—like her fears that they would not have enough money for food, for example.

I then said that this also had to do with boundaries—it was as though Carol could not distinguish between inner feelings and outer happenings. Thus she feared that Eric's bad feelings would get inside her and make her bad. Eric seemed to share this fear, since he was worried that the therapists would be invaded by his cold virus.

The session ended with Eric talking about a row they had nearly had the previous night. He had been too tired to talk to her, and Carol had immediately interpreted this as evidence that he had been seeing an ex-lover.

This session vividly reveals the couple's mutual anxieties about spilling out and not being contained. Both partners lacked any secure sense of their own internal space. Carol alternatively felt that Eric was going to invade her with his badness or that she would get inside him, feel trapped (as with her parents), and have to get out. Outside, though, the world was full of unpredictable dangers. When she could not get inside Eric (because he was tired or doing something else), she immediately felt that he must be getting inside someone else. This relationship typified the container/contained type of relationship described by Jung, with the caveat that, in this case, the container, Eric, was himself too fragile to be able to offer containment for his often panic-stricken wife (Jung, 1925; Lyons & Mattinson, 1993). He felt alternately invaded by or emptied out by her and sought containment elsewhere—in the pub or in his affair. Each attempted to use the relationship with the other as their own ego boundary but then felt they were contaminated by or contaminating the other.

At bottom, these anxieties were concerned with fears of disintegration and loss of being. This was vividly portrayed when they tried to re-mortgage their house to pay off their debts and were unable to do so because a surveyor had found a structural crack in it. While there was plenty of evidence of intrusive identification between them, I believe that their lack of ego boundaries was not merely the result of intrusive identification, but also the underlying cause for which intrusive identification was utilized as an attempted remedy.

Development of internal space

Klein's original model of projective identification assumes the existence of an internal space bounded by the physical body into which objects can be introjected and out of which they are projected (Klein, 1946). Psychic processes are regarded as the mental representations of physical events: thus, Klein sees introjection and projection as phantasies corresponding to the actual process of taking in food and excreting waste matter. The early ego is, to paraphrase Freud, a stomach ego.

This model has been modified by later developments in Kleinian thought in ways that were also anticipated by Winnicott (1960a, 1960b). Firstly, there has been a greater recognition of the unintegration of the early ego. Secondly, there has been a greater emphasis on the social nature of the infant's early experience.

Bick's seminal paper on the experience of the skin emphasized the unintegrated state of the early ego, which is barely
unable to hold itself together. In the absence of the holding
environment provided by the mother, the infant has to resort to
the defensive measures of "second-skin" holding (Bick, 1968).
Eric's eczema and the anxieties associated with it seem to be a
quite concrete manifestation of this state in which the ego
boundary, represented by the skin, is inadequate to act as a
container for the infant's extreme vulnerability and helplessness. Eric's fear of "giving something away" represents a fear of
losing his sense of self.

Here containment is meant in quite literal terms—i.e. the
need for a limiting membrane, initially provided by the mother's
holding function, which protects the baby in a good-enough way
from fears of spilling out and disintegrating.

In this model, projective identification is not a possibility at
first, since there is no secure sense of the inside to be projected
out of. Any event, whether internal or external, can become a
noxious threat to the fragile continuity of the infant's sense of its
own existence if the infant is not securely held (Winnicott,
1960a). Therefore projection, the phantasy of putting outside
that which is inside, even if it were possible, would be no solution. The primary anxiety is the fear of annihilation. Winnicott
recognized that the early sense of self is so vulnerable and fragile
that it can be—and often is—temporarily snuffed out by the loss
of maternal holding (Winnicott, 1967).

Bion's model of the origin of thought with his notion
of "thoughts without a thinker" also moves away from the assumption of a pre-existent ego with an already developed sense
of internal space (Bion, 1962b). The sense of internal space is
exactly what has to be established through the process of containment. For Bion, containment refers to the process whereby
beta elements are transformed into alpha elements through the
processes of projection, digestion within the mother, and re-
introjection by the infant (Bion, 1962a). Although he retains the
alimentary metaphor of Kleinian meta-psychology—note the
stomach–ego analogy implied by the metaphor of "digestion"—
he uses these concepts to describe something altogether more
abstract. The effect of containment is to confer *meaning* on
the infant's raw mental experience. Containment refers to the

way in which the mother inducts the infant into the human community.

Winnicott also refers to the creation of meaning, but he dispenses with the alimentary metaphor. He describes the way in which the infant makes a "gesture" that is recognized and responded to by the mother. This renders the world meaningful to the infant in terms of his own omnipotent power to create it (Winnicott, 1960b). Although this meaning is, in part, illusory, it is not *only* a phantasy, since it depends so much on the active participation of the mother. It is the result of a communication within a relationship that promotes the infant's sense of self via the maintenance of a sense of agency, continuity, and satisfaction, for example.

Initially, then, the infant experiences its whole world as its container (cf. "the world is my oyster"); gradually, the experience of frustration introduces the awareness of a world outside the container, and the container shrinks to form the boundary of ego-identity. Important vestiges of early omnipotence remain, however, in the experience of transitional objects and transitional phenomena—external objects that are saturated with personal meaning to the extent that they can no longer be thought of as purely external (Winnicott, 1951). Winnicott regards the capacity to relate in this intermediate area as essential to creative living (Winnicott, 1967). Here I wish to draw attention to the implication that creative living implies the capacity to maintain fluid ego boundaries without losing a sense of one's own separate self. This has great significance for couple relationships—a point to which I return at the end of the chapter.

I would like to make a further link between Bion and Winnicott by suggesting that the infant's gestures *arise from* beta elements and represent that aspect of the latter which Bion designates as "evacuation", but which might, rather, be regarded as spontaneous expression of proto-mental stimulation; as Winnicott might say, an expression of the undifferentiated psyche–soma (Winnicott, 1960a). Like beta elements, the infant's gestures are proto-communications that cannot become communications as such until they are recognized by the mother. It is an over-simplification to think of the infant, or indeed the adult, projecting with the deliberate albeit unconscious purpose of communicating its experience to the mother/

analyst. My clinical experience suggests that while I may learn a great deal about patients from the countertransference experiences they elicit, this is not necessarily intentional on their part. The infant does not project in order to be understood: understanding is a function of the relationship.

In my view, projective identification is the wrong metaphor for this process and can be misleading. We need to think of this early form of communication not as projective identification from ego to containing object, but as an interactional field. The infant's gesture is the expression of a beta element, but it is not a projection; it is an event within the interactional field of the mother–infant relationship. Gesture and response form the context for one another, as do container and contained. The mother's recognition creates a sense for the infant that "I am in the world" (my gesture is recognized, I exist) but also "the world is in me" (mother's response forms the matrix for my own set of personal meanings). That is: "I am both the container and the contained." This two-way relationship is also the basis for our entry into the wider social world of language.

The mother's reverie—the means by which she receives the infant's gesture and gives it meaning—is dependent on the fluidity of her own ego boundaries: she identifies with the infant but does not lose her own sense of separate existence. Indeed, the word "communication" comes from the Latin root *communis* meaning "common"—that is, "belonging equally to more than one".

Communication and containment in the couple relationship

I now wish to draw together the implications of the preceding theoretical discussion for couple relationships.

It is apparent that in a couple such as Eric and Carol, these early processes of containment have gone badly awry. Both of them felt filled with a sense of despair that the other would be able to recognize their gestures. This despair frequently invaded the therapists' countertransference and infected our relationship with one another, so that we each tended to pursue our own course separately and were unable to support one another. It may be a legacy of this countertransferential phenomenon that my co-therapist does not feature in the clinical material described above. During the final year of our work with Eric and Carol, we were able to make considerable headway in addressing this countertransference problem; undoubtedly our increased capacity to support and value one another reflected—and perhaps initiated—comparable changes in the couple.

It was as though their relationship constituted not only a repeated re-enactment of the original failure of containment, *but an exaggeration and exacerbation of it due to the defences against it.* Eric's denial and Carol's volatility involved omnipotent attempts to obliterate and evacuate their painful sense of deprivation—especially in connection with their continual financial anxiety. Thus each of them had to cope not only with a primitive beta element proto-communication from the other, which itself would be more than they could be expected to contain, but also with the loading of these communications with the painful desperation of their previous failure to be recognized and the defences against that pain—splitting, denial, and the evacuative use of projective identification. Of course, by its very nature projective identification further undermines ego boundaries and the capacity for self-containment, but, as I said earlier, I do not believe this to be the primary cause of the problem.

As an aside, I might mention that this touches on the long-standing debate between deficit and defence theories of narcissism. I have come to the point where I can no longer understand this argument, since I cannot conceive of narcissistic defences except in relation to some sense of deficit, nor any deficit that will not produce a defence. In clinical work we always see a mixed picture. While it may not be enough simply to offer a holding environment in which patients can regress and experience being understood—a criticism sometimes levelled against Winnicott by those of a Kleinian persuasion—it is also not enough to interpret the destructive aspects of narcissism without acknowledging the existential anxieties with which they are associated.

In relation to Eric and Carol, the therapists tended to divide on this issue—especially in relation to Carol's destructive outbursts, where I would tend to go for robust confrontation while

my co-therapist tended to stress her sense of not being recognized and acknowledged. On one or two occasions I became
openly angry myself, interpreting her outbursts as destructive
attacks against the therapy as well as against Eric. In fact, these
direct responses did make a positive difference to Carol, but
they were much easier—and safer—to make in a foursome,
where I could rely on my co-therapist to retain a sympathetic
sense of Carol's desperation. Gradually we each became more
able to integrate both aspects in our interpretations. When the
couple ended therapy, Carol gave us a thank-you card, on which
she wrote, "I will hear your words in my head and they will stay
with me—even when you were cross!" In order to communicate
with Carol, it was necessary to set a very firm boundary that
took account both of the original gesture that had not been met
and of the defensive response against it. This is reminiscent of
the importance that Frances Tustin gives to intervening firmly to
prevent the patient making use of autistic defences against
communication (Tustin, 1986).

While Eric and Carol presented primarily a lack of boundaries, other couples who share a similar experience of early
failure of containment may present with defensive, over-rigid,
but brittle boundaries, combined with fears of intrusion and
incorporation. Typically, each feels controlled and dominated by
the other. These are the false-self couples (Fisher, 1993) caught
up in re-enactments of the infant's experience of being filled up
with the mother's projections or, in Winnicott's terms, where
"the mother substitutes her own gesture which is to be given
sense by the compliance of the infant" (Winnicott, 1960b, p.
145). There is a critical difference here between a mother whose
ego boundaries are fluid enough to include her infant within
them and a mother who maintains a narcissistic relation to the
infant in which the infant is used as a vehicle for her own
projections.

In all these couples, the fundamental anxiety is with the
preservation of the self. Projective identification is used in two
ways. In the first place, it may be used as a means of evacuation,
in an attempt to get rid of noxious beta elements consisting of
misunderstood gestures, anxieties not responded to, and confusing elements introduced by the other. All of these things

threaten the partners' fragile sense of personal existence. Tragically, evacuation by one constitutes confusion and intrusion for the other, creating an escalating vicious circle.

This leads on to the second use of projective identification: as an attempt to get inside the other or incorporate the other inside the self. This leads to the state of projective gridlock described by Morgan (chapter two). Here I wish only to underscore the desperate urgency to find a container that generates this kind of omnipotent projective identification. In my view, intrusive identification can best be understood as a defence against the threat of annihilation, which is also what I take Bion to refer to as "nameless dread".

These uses of projective identification need to be clearly distinguished from the classic situation of a mutual projection system in which each partner carries some split-off aspect of the other—the sort of situation in which it is possible to talk about partners "marrying their other half". Such individuals have been able to establish a secure internal space with a defined ego boundary but only on condition that the more problematic aspects of themselves are split off. Unlike couples with no boundaries or defensive "second-skin" rigid boundaries, these couples know who they are and what they are like—or they think they do. When they meet an other who is like the disowned parts of themselves, they may experience a faint stirring of recognition, but in the couples who come for therapy, this early recognition of the self in the other has been buried by the anxiety it arouses and the renewed use of projective identification to defend against it. Therapeutic work is directed towards elucidating what is actually shared between the couple as a means of re-opening the potential channels of communication and containment that have been blocked by mutual projective identification.

Conclusion: mutual identification

Finally, I want to return to the question I raised at the beginning of this chapter. What might couple relationships look like where the interaction is not dominated by projective identification?

It is here that the distinction between identification and projective identification is necessary. Couples choose each other on the basis of a mutual identification: "I like you because you are like me." Where there is a capacity to make an identification *without losing the sense of one's own identity and, by implication, confusing the self with the other*, couples are then able to create a sense of "us" that acts as the third factor—the relationship that contains them (Colman, 1993). This formulation has an advantage over the usual account of unconscious choice in that it is inclusive of arranged marriages where the mutual identification is more on the basis of socio-cultural factors than individual psychological ones, although these factors play a considerably greater part in romantic marriage than its social idealization is willing to acknowledge.

In order for this mutual identification to develop between the couple, the partners need to be capable of the same kind of fluid ego boundaries as is the mother in responding to her infant's gesture. To some extent this fluidity is an ordinary factor of daily life in which there are many situations where ego boundaries are not co-terminous with the skin boundary. To take a simple example: if I am driving my car and an accident occurs, I am likely to say that "someone went into the back of *me*". While I am in the car, my sense of my physical boundaries extends outwards to the boundary of the vehicle. Once I leave the car, it becomes once again an external object, albeit it may be one in which I have an emotional investment. I think this relationship could certainly be described as an identification, but it has none of the features or motivations normally associated with projective identification—it is neither communication, nor evacuation, nor defence, although I suppose it could be described as a form of object relationship. At any rate, having well-established ego boundaries does not mean that they are fixed and solid: the capacity for a fluid extension and retraction of one's own personal boundary is, in fact, a sign of mental health and internal security. It is also the basis for communication with others, the experience of a relationship in common, belonging equally to more than one.

Highly narcissistic individuals in whom ego boundaries are poorly established are unable to manage either the extension or the retraction. To pursue the analogy of the car: these are the people who place in their rear windows the sign: "You toucha my car, I smasha your face." Damage to the car is experienced as damage to the self. Alternatively, such individuals may be unable to make any investment in external objects or even in their own bodies, which are treated as mere machines.

It is, of course, highly problematic when such means of relating are extended to personal relationships. Unless the ego boundary can be safely extended to include the other, it is not possible to feel that kind of mutual recognition which makes couple relationships worth the candle—in other words, to experience the relationship as a container in which gestures are received and understood, reinforcing the individual's sense of personal existence and value.

Yet if the extended boundary cannot be withdrawn or cannot be distinguished from one's private internal space which remains intact, then the partner cannot be allowed any autonomy, or such autonomy is experienced as a personal insult—a rent in the fabric of one's own internal container.

I want to suggest that the basis of unconscious partner choice is not only projective identification, but also a sense of *resonance* with another, the experience of recognition of the self in the other which allows the self to grow, almost literally, in that it involves an expansion of one's ego boundary to include the experience of the other. Of course, in practice these two different forms of identification (projective and non-projective) are likely to occur side by side. The essential difference is that while projective identification diminishes the self, positive identification with another enhances it. Some readers might argue that this distinction merely refers to whether introjection or projection is dominant in the psychic economy.

For me, this still has the disadvantage of implying a wholly separate self into which experiences are introjected. I prefer the notion of an interactive field in which the multiple gestures of each partner take on a host of private meanings, which are shared between the couple, continually reinforcing the sense of personal existence, identity, and value and leading to mutual growth.

CHAPTER FIVE

Identity and intimacy in the couple: three kinds of identification

James Fisher

In thinking about the adult couple, it is common to talk about the capacity for *intimacy* as a mark of the maturity of relating. It is sometimes contrasted with *autonomy* (as in Cleavely, 1993) and sometimes seen to include the capacity for separateness, as in Colman's discussion of the *internal capacity for marriage*:

> Another way of putting this would be to describe it as the capacity for intimacy, since *intimacy implies differentiation and separation*: the sharing of our innermost being with another.

He then goes on to say:

> Without separateness, intimacy becomes conflated with fusion: many couples cannot feel intimate unless they feel the same as their partner. . . . In fact, because they cannot tolerate separateness, they cannot achieve intimacy either and are therefore condemned to the sterile coldness of isolation. . . . [Colman, 1993, pp. 132f; italics added]

In this chapter I would like to explore the experience of intimacy from a psychoanalytic point of view. It is interesting that much of contemporary discussion in psychoanalysis about the analytic relationship in the consulting-room between analyst and patient, especially in the Kleinian and post-Kleinian tradition, is concerned with the difficulties of establishing and maintaining emotional contact. In a sense it is a discussion of intimacy and the capacity for it, as well as the ways in which it is blocked, attacked, perverted, or destroyed. One could say that the analytic setting is an important "laboratory" for the exploration of the nature of intimate relating.

It is hardly surprising, therefore, that we turn to psychoanalysis for an understanding of intimacy. We could add that psychoanalytic psychotherapy with couples is an attempt to bring the adult couple into that "laboratory", where observing and understanding can be part of a process of growth and change in the capacity for emotional contact.

Rather than starting my discussion of intimacy with a view that it is necessarily something to be desired, I would like to begin with a definition of intimacy purely in terms of distance, taking my cue from Meltzer's analysis of the topic.

> I want to use the word "intimacy" in a manner free from implication as to the quality, emotionality, of a relationship, but only having reference to social distance. From this point of view, its limits, on a spectrum, would be isolation on the one hand and fusion on the other. . . . Between the two extremes lies a broad band of variations in intimacy and, I am suggesting, sincerity. In other words, I am trying to investigate this quality of social contact free of moral bias that would view it as a virtue. [Meltzer, 1971/1994, p. 261]

Starting from this minimalist definition, I want to explore how an understanding of identification and the related "sense of identity" can illuminate different kinds or qualities of "intimacy. This resembles in some ways Colman's emphasis on separateness as a prerequisite for intimacy, although in this chapter it is not separateness *per se* that is at issue but the nature of the "sense of identity". In Meltzer's recently published book-length essay on "sincerity" (Meltzer, 1971/1994), he describes three broad types of identification, and he uses his analysis of the quality of "sincerity", I suggest, to identify three types of "intimacy". I am not claiming that this was his intention, nor that he would agree with my analysis of, and use of, what he has written. In this chapter I follow on and develop some themes from my earlier examination of Meltzer's notion of the "claustrum" (Fisher, 1994), although what I say here is not dependent on a reading of that paper.

What I say in this chapter is not particularly new, although I do want to use terms such as "infantile" in a particular way in order to try to illuminate the various experiences and kinds of "intimacy" we encounter in couples. The reader may thus encounter familiar ideas in an unfamiliar guise. I have found these ideas helpful in thinking about my clinical experiences, and I invite the reader to rethink with me the links between intimacy and one's sense of identity. I shall be thinking primarily about how one's sense of identity shapes the intimacy that is possible with someone else, although it is true that the intimacy one experiences shapes one's sense of identity.

If I were to put my thesis in a schematic form, it would look like this. *First*, there are *infantile identifications*, which are at the heart of the experience of emotion and lead to an *infantile sense of identity*. This sense of identity leads to the possibility of a corresponding *infantile intimacy*, which is the very heart of the intimate couple relationship insofar as intimacy is an emotional experience. *Secondly*, there are *narcissistic identifications* (primarily projective and adhesive identification), which lead to a *delusion of identity*, along with a consequent *delusion of intimacy*. *Finally*, there are *introjective identifications*, which, when the introjective identification is with the "internal parental couple" or what is sometimes called the "combined object", make possible an *adult sense of identity*. This is characterized by a sense of humility, gratitude, aspiration, and concern for the other, which makes possible a *mature intimacy*—something to which we aspire and for which, when we experience it, we feel a sense of gratitude.

In this chapter I want to explore these ideas both theoretically and in clinical experience with couples. Following some further theoretical points in this introduction, I will report a lengthy excerpt from two sessions with one couple. The reason for this lengthy material is my wish to illustrate moments when one can see evidence of differing states of mind. Of course, the three kinds of sense of identity do not occur in a "pure" form but oscillate from moment to moment in a way that makes it difficult to recognize them. I shall then discuss that material, along with some other material from other couples, in the three main sections of the chapter.

One of our assumptions might be that a firm sense of identity is a prerequisite for intimacy between two people, and in a sense that is true, especially when we are talking about mature object relating. However, on inspection we shall see that there can be several ways in which a sense of identity can arise, all of which can result in a "firm"—even though sometimes momentary— sense of identity. In fact, Rosenfeld, Steiner, and others have shown how a narcissistic organization of the personality can be not only "firm" but fixed and rigid (Rosenfeld, 1971; Steiner, 1993).

The more important consideration, I suggest, is the quality or nature of the sense of identity. It is this relationship between identity and intimacy that I want to explore, as well as the three broad types of both identity and intimacy. As I said, the first has to do with momentary experiences of a sense of identity deriving from infantile parts of the personality vis-à-vis internal and external objects with which they are linked. I have in mind here a spontaneous experience of emotion connected with an object with which it is linked. Here "infantile" is not used in some pejorative sense by way of contrast with mature or adult but, rather, to indicate a spontaneous occurrence of emotion vis-à-vis an object such as one observes in the immediacy of the infant's experience. As such, it is the core of all emotion we experience, whether as a child or as an adult. To deny one's infantile aspects would be to reject the capacity for emotion. And in Bion's elegant analysis of the nature of the mind, being able to experience emotion is the way the mind mysteriously grows and develops—or in his enigmatic language, the alpha function that transforms sense-data into alpha elements available for dreaming and thinking (Bion, 1962b).

In the exploration of the variability of a sense of identity that arises from the infantile parts of the personality, we shall see that, while the momentary sense of identity is characterized by spontaneity, there is no stable or integrated sense of identity. The momentary sense of identity, however, is marked by "sincerity", due to its link with, or expression of, emotion. This sincerity, with its depth of emotionality, stands in sharp contrast to the emotional "shallowness" that accompanies the denial of the existence of infantile structures and the internal objects with which they are closely linked (Meltzer, 1971/1994). This can be seen in the latency child as well as in the conventionality of the settled adult, with their social carapace and the adaptational quality of the relationships of both.

The second type of identification and consequent sense of identity arises out of the anxieties of this fragile infantile sense of identity and is, in fact, a defence against those anxieties. It is a delusional sense of identity based in narcissistic identification, the most familiar of which is what Melanie Klein came to call "projective identification". Adhesive identification is another form of narcissistic identification, the identification characteristic of social adaptation and conformity. In my discussion of this delusional sense of identity, however, I focus on projective identification—the form of narcissistic identification that has been extensively investigated in psychoanalytic writings over the past thirty years or so (see Ruszczynski, chapter one).

One question I am particularly interested to consider is the issue of Bion's description of the dynamics of projective identification as a form of non-verbal communication. Is he using the term "projective identification" in Melanie Klein's sense, or is he, in fact, talking about a quite different kind of "projective identification"? This issue is similar to that raised by Colman (chapter four) when he talks about a process of relating that, I suggest, may be more closely related to the first kind of identification and the infantile sense of identity.

The third type of sense of identity is that of the adult part of the personality, which Meltzer sees as related to introjective identification—what he has described as "the most important and most mysterious concept in psychoanalysis" (Meltzer, 1978, p. 459). This is perhaps the most important aspect of Meltzer's systematic structural metapsychology, one that calls for a more intensive exposition than is possible in the context of this chapter. The introjection here is not related to just any object but is, rather, the introjective identification with the internal combined object, the internal parental couple, initially in part-object terms but ultimately in whole-object coital relationship. Both Di Ceglie (chapter three) and O'Shaughnessy (1993), among others, have

written about the consequences when what is introjected remains at the part-object level, never reaching the quality of the
mature internal parental couple or combined object.

In order to illustrate some aspects of these three types of
"sense of identity" and the corresponding kinds of "intimacy", I
want to look at excerpts from two sessions with a couple a co-
therapist and I saw in therapy for some time whom I call "Mr and
Mrs P". Later I refer to material from other couples, whom I saw
with other co-therapists. I am indebted to these co-therapists for
access to notes that I have used along with mine to reconstruct
the material reported. There are many ways this material could
be taken up, but in the discussion that follows I focus on what
we might describe as the emergence of a varying "sense of
identity" appearing at different moments in the sessions and
how they relate to the kinds of intimacy (or lack of it) that is
available to the couple in those moments.

Claustrum nightmares

MR AND MRS P

Mrs P had begun the session by describing a television pro-
gramme she had watched, in which a psychologist specializ-
ing in perversions had compared bondage with love. As Mrs P
heard it, bondage and love were alike in that in both it was
necessary to have complete confidence in your partner because you feel so vulnerable. This led into a discussion of
"intimacy" in which Mr P commented that he didn't know
much about the bondage scene, but he had always thought it
had to do with people getting pleasure out of pain. The pain
had to be borne in order to achieve some satisfaction. I
observed that in the light of his comments in recent sessions
this sounded a bit like a description of his experience of
therapy. Mrs P laughed and went on to describe a book she
had been reading, in which the author was collating different
accounts of the suicide of the subject of the book. She was
especially interested in one view, which suggested that the
widow had been responsible by pushing him into it. The
different stories reminded her of how she and Mr P so often

had radically differing versions of the same event—something we often commented on. My co-therapist suggested that it sounded as if she were sitting in judgement on the characters in the book, and perhaps she experienced us as sitting in judgement on them in the session. She observed that it was difficult to think of us as real people, since we give so little of ourselves away. She said she knew that there are certain rules in therapy with which they have to comply, and gradually they are discovering these rules they have to play by. We suggested that it was as if she had to be emotionally cut off in therapy and experienced us as being that way as well.

Mr P was reminded of when he used to fence, and how difficult it was to fence with a stranger—aware unconsciously of our fencing with Mrs P, as we often seemed to do. He pointed out that it was necessary to know your opponent, because you had to trust him in such a dangerous sport. Even if you were properly dressed, with plenty of padding, you could get hurt; blood could be drawn. I commented that he seemed to be talking about a kind of "intimacy" that was dangerous, in which one was as vulnerable as in the "bondage" Mrs P had talked about. Talking about being vulnerable in close relationships led Mr P on to a description of how vulnerable he had felt in his own family as a child, and how he had to get far away from his family, as had Mrs P from her family. Rather poignantly, he added that his children can be too demanding, just like his parents. Even though he loves them, the more you give children, the worse and more demanding they become. What followed was a prolonged and tense argument between them on this subject, which at one point we linked with their outstanding bill and their feelings about our continuous "demand" for money from them.

At the end of the session I commented that there had been plenty of fencing between them, as indeed there had been some between them and us, and although in some ways they were "well padded", there seemed to have been the occasional "touch". The dangers of this game were real, and it even seemed that it could end in death or suicide for them. I added that they both seem imprisoned in this "game" and in the rules of the game. Just as the session was ending, Mrs P asked how they were to escape from this prison. Both seemed in despair as they left.

In the next session we heard about a dream Mr P had had and then an associated couple story—a story that, like most such "stories" in therapy, can be analysed as a "couple dream". Both of these dreams told us about the unconscious phantasy of th^ "bondage" world of "fencing" in which they were imprisoned and from which they felt there was no escape. Mr P spoke about having eaten very late the night before with friends, which resulted in their both having had nightmares and a disturbed night because of the food. Mrs P couldn't recall her dreams, but Mr P told us that in his dream *everything was violent and aggressive and he was being pursued by gangs. Someone was attacking him with a hypodermic needle, and it was infected.*

Mrs P broke in to remind us that I had mentioned murder in the previous session. Mr P went on to say that in the dream *someone had stabbed him in the side, but the needle broke because he was wearing his heavy waxed country walking coat.* He added that there were gangs on the street, child prostitution, heroin dealing—all quite unbelievable.

I commented on Mrs P's linking the dream with our talk of suicide and death last week and supposed that that must have meant "murder" to her. While we were trying to understand that connection with them, Mrs P mentioned their son's playing with a "hypodermic" syringe, squirting water on everyone. Mr P responded sharply that hypodermics were not very pleasant objects—a thought that led on to a story about his mother's death. Mother and father had both received an inoculation, and, as far as they could trace it, this led to both parents getting hepatitis. Mother died of complications from it soon after. Father recovered, but with a severely damaged liver—eventually dying from internal bleeding, as had Mr P's mother.

Mr P also talked about the coat that in the dream felt like a suit of armour, noting that it was in fact the coat Mrs P had bought for him. Her retort was that it was the one he tried to lose, while he insisted that on the contrary, he really loved that coat. Mrs P linked this talk about the coat to the padding for fencing Mr P was talking about in the previous session.

I commented that the thoughts in the previous session seemed persecuting, to judge from the nightmares, linking that with my comments in the previous session about how cut-off emotionally she was. Mrs P responded that some of the things said the previous week had indeed bothered her and linked her being emotionally cut off with her experience as a child, when she had not been allowed to go out. The only option she had had was to "go into herself". Her parents had not even liked her to read, so she had just had to survive in her inner world, which no one knew about. Outwardly she had been silent. At home it had been like being in a prison; she described her childhood home as "without a garden". Her boarding school, too, had been like a prison, with its incredibly complicated set of rules. Again she had had to survive by being on her own in her inner world, which no one knew about.

Later in the session we heard that the setting in the dream was a house that belonged to a friend in another country, where they had often visited him. The two of them then described this friend as very nervous and "paranoid" about attacks, so the house had no door-bell. People would have to telephone or fax to say they were at the door, and then he would come down and let them in. They pointed out that it was a bit like a gothic fortress—quite a huge, impressive building, with staircases everywhere, cellars, tall windows, and shutters.

Together they went on to tell us a story of a terrifying experience. They had once arrived at this friend's house just after midnight, having intended to get there earlier. They called up in the middle of a cold and snowy night, but somehow the friend did not hear the telephone. Suddenly they were surrounded by police pointing guns at them. The children were terrified. The police had thought they were terrorists because British royalty were visiting the city. The police then escorted them out of the centre of the city, saying they were in great danger, and finally they spent the rest of the night in the camper van, hidden on a building-site.

Infantile sense
of identity and intimacy

There are many aspects of this material that could be taken up. Here, however, I am interested in the question of intimacy and the relationship to kinds of identification. I should make it clear that I am not suggesting that we can neatly isolate different kinds of identification operating in those sessions. The reality in the consulting-room is never quite so simple. What I want to point out are hints of different kinds of states of mind at different moments in the sessions, which can be illuminated by thinking about them in the ways I am suggesting.

First I want to mention what Meltzer describes as the "two metapsychological conditions for intimacy". It will be seen from these two conditions that they do not determine the quality of the intimacy, only the possibility of proximity. The first precondition of intimacy of contact is that it requires what Meltzer describes as "geographic contiguity in terms of unconscious phantasy". The second is that "the two parties must inhabit the same emotive world" (Meltzer, 1971/1994, p. 262). These conditions are so couched in the conceptual language of Meltzer's metapsychology that they require some "unpacking" before their significance can be made clear.

In order to track this understanding of intimacy, I want to look back to the sessions with Mr and Mrs P, to see whether this material can help to elaborate an understanding of the two conditions for intimacy, beginning with a consideration of infantile identification. There were times, for example, in the second session with Mr and Mrs P, when one had a sense of a spontaneous expression of infantile feeling—primarily with Mr P. In the recounting of his dream and in the associations to it, it was possible to have moments of contact with a little boy who was terrified of something intrusive that was dangerous and poisonous. There was part of the self identified with the friend who would "became hysterical" about the prospect of an "intruder", in Mr P's dream in the form of a "hypodermic needle".

At this point in the session Mrs P made a "needling" comment, reminding him of their son *playing* with a "hypodermic" syringe, which prompted his association to the death of his parents as the result of an inoculation. It seemed that he moved into a different state of mind, perhaps something connected with a little boy whose intrusiveness was linked with the death of his parents. I return to this when we consider narcissistic identification.

This infantile anxiety was in some way connected with the transference experience of the previous session, when my speaking about fears of death had felt to him as if he had been attacked by an infected "hypodermic" that got under his skin. Both my co-therapist and I had a strong sense that Mr P had made a strong emotional link with me during this stage of the therapy—a link with unmistakable homosexual undertones. My words seemed to be a kind of food, which became confused with an infected "hypodermic" penis.

There were only a few moments in the session when it felt that we had an emotional link with Mrs P, where her sense of identity seemed to be that of a child/baby retreating into itself. Following my link between the previous session and something "indigestible" as well as something that must have "got under the skin", Mrs P seemed to abandon for a moment her narcissistic identification with us as therapists, in which she made "interpretations" to Mr P. She began to talk about her own childhood defence of going into herself, and for a brief moment she seemed to experience the infantile anxiety that lay behind the need for her defensive self-sufficiency. It was, however, momentary, and as she rehearsed the story of her boarding-school experience, we were left with the feeling of an all-too-familiar account that we had explored time and time again with her in therapy. She knew how to use her ability to cut off emotionally, read the rules of the game/boarding school/therapy environment, and say the right things in order to be accepted. What was almost impossible was the capacity to sustain some contact with the terrified, lonely, and excluded little girl.

But what of the "intimacy" between Mr and Mrs P at an infantile level? At the point Mr P introduced the story about his friend and the fortress-like scary medieval house, there seemed to be a link between them, as together they recounted the episode of the visit. When they came to the part about the terrifying police and the frightened children, she joined him in a lively way, which suggested that for a moment there was a kind of emotional link between them as frightened children. They were at that moment not like an adult parental couple, but more like "babes in the wood" themselves, terrified by threatening authority figures with "hypodermic needles" that had become "guns", and unable to gain entrance into a protective house. Instead, they were left to shelter on the site of an unfinished building. At that moment neither was safe in their therapy-house, because the authorities/therapists had been experienced as increasing their anxieties by their talk of death and murder. It is also true that the "babes-in-the-wood" can also be the "children-ganged-up-against-the-adults"—something we at times felt from them.

If there was a moment of an "intimacy of the infantile sense of identity" between them in this session, it was at this point, when they were united in telling us this terrifying tale. We might say that they were drawn together in their infantile anxieties in the face of their shared experience of anxieties occasioned by the previous session. This is not an uncommon experience in the therapy, and I can think of many times when a couple will have fleeting moments of shared intimacy vis-à-vis the therapist(s) as the "children-in-it-together".

Nevertheless, this is a kind of intimacy and, moreover, an important kind of intimacy. It includes the intimate contact not just of the "babes-in-the-wood" kind, but also the intimacy of the spontaneous, happy children at play. Any intimate relationship in which it is impossible to be infantile together at the same moment would be a seriously impoverished relationship.

It is important, however, to note here the limitations of what I am describing as the intimacy of the infantile sense of self. Infantile identifications are by their very nature fragmentary and momentary, as are the infantile parts of the self and the part-objects with which they are closely linked. Thus, for example, in the place of the contented infantile part of the self and the breast from which it obtains satisfaction, we can in another moment find an envious infantile part of the self attacking the internal mother's inside-babies with its damaging urine. Jealousy of siblings, moments of generosity, feelings of love or hate, or any of the myriad infantile emotions and states of mind can at any given time constitute the experience of the self, which can become available to self-consciousness and thus form the *sense of identity*.

The intimacy that is based on an infantile sense of identity requires that each partner to that intimacy meet in a shared arena of unconscious phantasy. In Meltzer's language, this means "geographical contiguity" in terms of the part-object linked with the infantile part of self, as well as occupying the same "emotive world"—that is, within or outside the sphere of good objects. We could say that this was what was happening when Mr and Mrs P met momentarily in a shared infantile intimacy vis-à-vis the therapists' words-as-dangerous-persecutors, a dilemma in which therapy became that frightening gothic house, both refuge and threat. But it was at most a fragmentary intimacy, destroyed almost immediately by the narcissistic intrusive identifications that formed a defence against the infantile anxieties.

Insofar as we can speak of an intimacy based on an infantile sense of self, we are talking about moments of an adult couple relationship. These moments, whether positive or negative, are important as moments of shared emotional intensity. They are too fragmentary and fluctuating, however, to define or to constitute a couple relationship. They are probably characteristic of even fleetingly casual contacts where infantile parts of the self and the other meet intensely and part with scarcely a farewell. Meltzer sums it up well:

> In both small children and adolescents, a great flux is present regarding the sense-of-identity, so that the different infantile parts are repeatedly seizing the organ of consciousness, and thus of communication. The result, momentarily, is often urgent, direct, and sincere communication, both of emotion and concerning emotion. But since the part in control changes very rapidly, taken over a period of time the communication may seem so full of contradictions as to approximate hypocrisy [Meltzer, 1971/1994, p. 264]

Meltzer points out that it is also the case that when a particular infantile part or organization of infantile parts is in control of consciousness, there can often be a sense of loneliness of a "child-in-the-adult-world". Attempts to obviate this sense of loneliness, such as the joining in adolescent gangs, can succeed to some extent, just as can the couple clinging together. But this can more often degenerate into something like narcissistic "gangs" that seek to obliterate infantile anxieties. When one is in touch with these infantile feelings, there can be a sense of fraud and humiliation that can be unbearable. Mr P struck my co-therapist and me as someone whose moments of emotional contact with us were so painful that he quickly retreated to his narcissistic defences—especially the "ivory tower" of his professional work, from which he could look down contemptuously at his wife's pleas that he spend more time with her. With Mrs P we had even fewer glimpses of the pain of her experience as a child-in-the-adult-world. Both described themselves as refugees, and indeed they were—refugees from the liveliness and painfulness of the infantile-life-in-the-family.

Another way of coping with these infantile anxieties is by denial of the existence of infantile structures and the internal objects with which they are linked. This denial can lead to a flattening of emotional experience and to a relating to the external world as well as to the partner in a "matter of fact" way. This produces a calculating, adaptive style, which, in Meltzer's words, "we read as 'shallow' for its lack of imagination, insensitivity to others' feelings, and materialism" (Meltzer, 1971/1994, p. 202). It is a pattern that we see in many couples who come to therapy, not to regain some contact with each other emotionally, but for assistance in re-establishing the denial of emotional reality, which has somehow broken down. Such a pattern of denial is almost always structured around narcissistic identifications.

Narcissistic identifications and intimacy

We might think that any process of narcissistic identification or any narcissistic sense of identity would preclude intimacy by definition. I should make clear the assumptions I am making in using the term "narcissistic", since usage varies significantly even within the psychoanalytic literature. I am assuming, in line with a tradition going back largely to Melanie Klein's early work, that the self experiences itself in terms of a relationship to an object, not in terms of an object-less impulse. "Narcissistic object relations" is not a contradiction in terms, but a way of indicating both the quality of relating and the object related to. That is, these are relationships of the self with part-objects which are important solely in terms of their function for the self (see Hinshelwood, 1991, pp. 354–359). It follows, then, that *projective identification is always a relationship with part-objects, never a whole object* in the Kleinian sense of "part-object" and "whole object". The reader can refer to Ruszczynski and Morgan (chapters one and two) for examples and discussions of narcissistic relating and the couple.

It will already be evident that any intimacy based on narcissistic identification will be a very one-sided intimacy indeed. In this part of the chapter I want to put narcissistic identification, and projective identification in particular, in the context of the three types of identification in order to consider the nature of the "intimacy" we observe with the sense of identity resulting from this second kind of identification.

One other theoretical point is of importance before we turn back to the clinical material for illustrations of this kind of "intimacy". When describing projective identification, we talk about parts of the self or internal objects that are split off and projected, with the result that the object is experienced as if it were identified with the split-off part or parts. We could think of this as the *content* of the omnipotent unconscious phantasy. It is, however, only one of the ways of describing this defence against anxiety. Meltzer, in the interview published in this book (chapter six), points out that Melanie Klein had in mind the *state of mind resulting from the omnipotent phantasy* of projective identification. I want to suggest that in some ways describing this *state of mind* can bring us closer to an understanding of the importance and the function of narcissistic identification than a description of what has been projected, although of course the two are closely related.

In the discussion that follows I refer inevitably to the contrast between the *state of mind* characteristic of projective identification and the *state of mind* characteristic of introjective identification. In a sense the one is what the other is not. Inevitably I discuss both and the contrast between them in this section and in the next, when I focus on introjective identification and the kind of intimacy it makes possible. I should also say that I am using the term "projective identification" to refer to the intrusive omnipotent unconscious phantasy that is closer to what Melanie Klein originally described (Klein, 1946). Meltzer uses the term "intrusive identification" for this (Meltzer, 1986). The term "projective identification" is now so embedded in our psychoanalytic vocabulary that it seems better to continue its use in this sense and to ask whether "projective identification" in, for example, Bion's sense might deserve a different name. In this I agree to some extent with Colman (chapter four) that the term "projective identification" can be confusing, because it is being used very broadly, although my analysis differs from his in a number of aspects. I return to this discussion at the end of this section.

What, then, characterizes the state of mind of someone who is in projective identification with an internal or an external object? The first observation is the most critical, and Meltzer states it clearly:

> In passing over from those aspects of sense-of-identity that derive directly from infantile structures to narcissistic identifications, we pass from psychic reality to delusion; from real identity, be it ever so fragmentary, to delusions of identity. [Meltzer, 1971/1994, p. 202]

Once this distinction is understood, much of the essential character of the state of mind of being in projective identification with an object becomes clearer. That is, we have moved from the psychic reality of infantile identifications to a *delusion* of identity. It could even be called a *con-fusion* of identity—that is, a "fusion with" something. One vital characteristic of delusion is *certainty*. There can be no doubt, no experience of learning, no learning from experience. What one "knows" is all there is to be known or all that is worth knowing. It is a state of mind marked by "the peculiar optimism, pomposity, and snobbish arrogance" of what Meltzer has described as the "delusion-of-clarity-of-insight" and the attitude of "sitting-in-judgement" (Meltzer, 1976).

Mrs P's identification with us as her therapists seemed to be a version of this, with its getting right inside our minds, which protected her, at least at times, from the unbearable infantile anxieties of being dependent on us. This familiar phenomenon could be seen in the acting-out characteristic of our experience with another couple, "Mr and Mrs Q".

MR AND MRS Q

My co-therapist and I had arranged to return to work early just for a session with them, so that the combination of our usual holiday break and their two-week holiday preceding that would not become an "intolerably" long break from therapy. As we might have anticipated, they missed that special session, leaving us sitting there on the last day of our holiday. Later Mrs Q reported an argument between them in which she thought that the date she had in mind that we had given them was when therapy resumed. However, "he was sure that therapists do not work during a holiday week". His delusional certainty swept her along until she, too, was certain that he was right.

We could, of course, note that the therapists' conscious intention to act in a caring way had led to what was in fact a "violation" of the boundary of the therapy—no doubt a kind of countertransference "acting-in". Here I only mean to call attention to Mr Q's *state of mind* and its effect on that of Mrs Q, who moved from her experience of thoughtful doubt to join him in his *certainty*. Perhaps the therapists' "acting-in" triggered infantile anxieties of dependence in Mr Q, which, in turn, led to his defensive projective identification with the minds of therapists whose content he *knew*.

With this description of the state of mind characteristic of projective identification, it is possible to recognize the state of mind even when we may be in doubt as to the nature of what is being projected. We might describe this as a descriptive or a "phenomenological" approach to narcissistic identifications, in contrast to a "dynamic" approach—that is, one that describes the content of the omnipotent phantasy. We may not always have access to the dynamics of the projective identification, the kind of unconscious phantasy that can leave its traces in the dreams patients bring. But the phenomenology of its presentation is often unmistakable. It is of course true that in most discussions of projective identification in the psychoanalytic literature there is a description of the state of mind as well as of what is projected. For example, Steiner writes:

We can see that projective identification gives rise to a state of mind in which true separateness is not experienced. This state of mind provides relief from anxiety and from frustration as well as from envy, and is idealised. [Steiner, 1993, p. 44]

We can see that the kind of "intimacy" that is possible in the face of this arrogant sense of identity has a peculiar quality. The first observation is that, like the delusional sense of identity, this is a *delusion of intimacy*. I think it is better to characterize it that way than to say simply that there is no intimacy. Mr and Mrs P, like many couples we see, are locked in something that keeps them in close proximity. Morgan (chapter two) has suggested the apt term "gridlock" for the kind of proximity in which these couples are bound. No doubt the "delusion of identity" is similar in some respects to what Winnicott (1960b) called the "false self". The "delusion of intimacy", therefore, is similar to what I have called the phenomenon of the "false self couple" (Fisher, 1993). Sometimes it seems more a "delusion of intimacy", and at other times more a "delusional intimacy", depending on one's vantage point.

In fact, the "intimacy" of couples like Mr and Mrs P does *at moments* meet the two conditions Meltzer describes for intimacy—a geographical contiguity in terms of the part-object with which they are in identification, as well as inhabiting the same emotive world. At other moments they can feel isolated from each other while in the presence of the other, because they either do not share an emotive world or one is "inside" an object while the other is "outside". It is the *delusion of intimacy*, oscillating with a corresponding *delusion of isolation*, which keeps them "grid-locked". Perhaps we could best describe the totality of this oscillation as collusion—that is, a kind of shared delusion. I shall offer just one brief example of something we often saw in our work with Mr and Mrs Q—a kind of "delusion of intimacy".

The central story of one session concerned them taking Mrs Q's car across town for repair at a garage that she knew. Mr Q was driving her car, and she was driving his. Although she was the one who knew where the garage was, Mr Q was driving ahead, Mrs Q following him. Of course, the inevitable happened. They got separated, losing each other in traffic. Mr Q, not knowing where to go, turned back and returned home. Mrs Q, however, carried on to the garage and sat there in the poignantly hopeless anticipation of his arrival. They could become "fused" in a shared delusion that was breathtaking in its certainty.

With Mr and Mrs Q, we could see the evidence of their state of mind and the "intimacy" they shared at such moments. However, in our sessions with Mr and Mrs P, we were also able occasionally to hear more of the detail of unconscious phantasies of this *delusional intimacy* when they shared their dreams and their associations to each other's dreams. For example, when Mr P seemed in touch with his infantile anxieties following his "homosexual" contact with me, he appeared to move into a projective identification with the father's dangerous potent penis as the infecting hypodermic needle. When Mrs P associated to his dream, recalling for us—*and for him*—the picture of a son "playing" with a "hypodermic syringe" by "squirting water on everyone", he then recounted for us a story of parents fatally infected by an injecting needle. Both parents died of "internal bleeding"—or, should we say, the internal parental couple attacked by an intrusive son. It seemed an omnipotent attack on the therapist couple as the externalized damaged internal couple. In the face of fears of retaliation by an infecting hypodermic in the dream, he found protection in the coat linked with Mrs P.

In the therapy it often felt as if the presence of Mrs P in the room for the most part deflected us from sustaining an emotional link with Mr P in order to explore his infantile anxieties. Mrs P, it seems, provided him with a "coat of armour" to protect him against, for example, homosexual anxieties. In his mind there was a kind of intimacy with her as a protective coat. If there was any genuine parental caring involved in this function, it was soon dispelled in the argument over whether he "loved" the coat or whether he tried to "lose" it. He was content to "use" her omnipotently, but he could not bear the anxiety of dependence on her in his fear that he, like his children and like his parents, would become too demanding.

A dream of Mrs P showed how she sought to use him in a similar way. In that dream:

> *Mrs P was giving a party. She had done all the work for it herself and was now entertaining her guests, taking round the food and drink. But every time she moved towards someone, her foot was trapped in the floor-boards, which seem to be rotten, with a lot of mess coming up through the damaged wood. She called for Mr P to help her, wanting to tell him that it was his responsibility to maintain the house. But he just went on chatting to people, taking no notice of her.*

Here, instead of a "coat" to protect him, she needs him to keep her from falling into the rotten mess underneath, or from being overwhelmed and trapped by the mess. Her internal structure is not secure, and there is a suggestion of confusion between oral/ feeding and the foot/penis/hand in the bottom. She presumably gets into this confusion as a result of her omnipotent wish to be the feeding breast, doing it all herself. It happens when the Mr P/brother/daddy figure (about whom we know from other dreams) is preoccupied with others, chatting to them and taking no notice of her or her plight. Mr P's version of why he could not help was revealed in the dream he told us in that same session, which also showed a failure of his omnipotence to steer things out of danger. In this dream:

> *The two of them were on a river-boat going down a fast-flowing, wide river, with high mountains on either side. There were magnificent cities on the banks as they passed. Then the boat turned into a side tributary, which seemed very steep, almost like a cascade* [mentioning a name of a city where he thought it might be, the name of which is associated with smells]. *He said it was hard to struggle to make progress, not frightening but as though the task of propelling the boat upstream was almost not worth doing because it seemed so impossible.*

Here the "geography" suggests that the two are together on a fast trajectory that takes them down from the beauty and magnificence of the head/breast, turning into the cascade of the urethral/anal area (the smells). From there it is an almost impossible task omnipotently to propel them back up. This recalls Meltzer's description of the mobility between the compartments of the internal mother's body in the claustrum (Meltzer, 1992, Fisher, 1994). What she wants from him in her dream, he feels to be impossible in his dream. A dream, he said, was associated with strong feelings which he could not articulate.

This is in marked contrast to a common experience in therapy when one of the couple is "reduced" to an infantile sense of identity, overcome, for example, by a sense of helplessness or anxiety, and the other can become the caring, comforting "parent" or "older sibling". In fact, it is a common complaint that one partner says the other can only listen or be sympathetic when he or she is "reduced to tears". A listening, caring intimacy when they are on a more equal footing seems almost impossible for these couples.

It may be that in the situation that I have just described, where one partner is "reduced" to an infantile sense of identity vis-à-vis the other, there may be a sense in which there is intimacy, but it may also be a kind of pseudo-intimacy, where the other has assumed a "pseudo-parental" role via projective identification. The state of mind produced by the projective identification with a parenting function will then be more of a self-righteous sense of superiority, often secretly scorning the infantile "weakness" of the partner and exploiting it to reinforce an omnipotent "pseudo-adult" sense of self. A genuine capacity to "parent" the other in moments of intimacy, when it is possible to reveal an infantile sense of identity to the other while needing the other to be parental, is dependent on an adult sense of identity in that other, which, in turn, is dependent on an introjection of a combined whole-object parental-couple-in-coitus. We return to this shortly.

There is, of course, a nearly infinite variety of combinations and permutations on this kind of collusion. Meltzer describes one as a "doll's-house" type of marriage, where "a sort of continual honeymoon exists and love is wonderful—I love me and you love me" (Meltzer, 1971/1994, p. 262). At another time, I would like to continue this exploration of types of collusion or delusion of intimacy, since it is important for the practice of psychoanalytic psychotherapy that we have a clear descriptive phenomenology of narcissistic collusion.

MR AND MRS R

In over three years of therapy with "Mr and Mrs R", we could never get through a session without each contemptuously dismissing the other, whether it was what one said or meant or intended. Even on a day when Mr R was celebrating his birthday and both of them were desperate to preserve a temporary truce, it degenerated at one point into one of her most dismissive and contemptuous attacks on him for his personal hygiene, in response to what she felt was his rejection of her in favour of one of his children from a previous marriage the evening before. Yet it was this couple who from time to time would describe brief periods of intense, highly sexualized ecstasy together in what they called their "Nirvana" times, the experience they shared at the beginning of the relationship. In those periods they were united in an excited closeness that we thought of as a kind of "fusion". Although we had no access to dreams that might have revealed some of the contours of the unconscious geography of that state, one can imagine that we were hearing about a state of mind consequent on an intrusion in unconscious phantasy into the genital compartment of the internal mother's genital. The shared excitement was evidence of a "delusion of intimacy". When they slipped out of that state of mind into the battle for survival in their relentless sadomasochistic duel, we similarly could imagine that we were hearing about the unconscious phantasy of intrusion into the compartment of the internal mother's rectum, where they were locked in that claustrum in a different "delusion of intimacy" (see Meltzer, 1992, or Fisher, 1994, for a description of this). It was a proximity that they could not bear, but from which they could not imagine an escape.

At this point, however, I want to return to an issue that I mentioned earlier—the kind of "projective identification" Bion had in mind in his description of the container/contained relationship (Bion, 1959). His development of this notion has become fundamental for contemporary psychoanalytic thinking. It has also, however, led to an expanded use of the term "projective identification", perhaps, as Colman (chapter four) suggests, too broad a use. Meltzer himself is clear that Bion is talking about a different kind of projective identification when he describes it as an unconscious phantasy "implementing the non-lexical aspects of language and behaviour, aimed at communication rather than action" (Meltzer, 1986, p. 69). In his interview in this book, Meltzer suggests that in using the term "projective identification" for this form of non-verbal communication, Bion was making a "tactical not a theoretical error" (see chapter six).

I do not want to review here Bion's discussion of the container/contained relationship, which is in any case by now quite familiar. It seems to me that if we consider projective identification not from the point of view of what I have called the "dynamic" aspects but, rather, from the point of view of the phenomenology of the state of mind characteristic of one who is in projective identification with an object, we may have a way of distinguishing a narcissistic sense of identity from an infantile sense of identity. Consider, for example, Bion's original and now classic description of the container/contained relationship:

> The analytic situation built up in my mind a sense of witnessing an extremely early scene. I felt that the patient had experienced in infancy a mother who dutifully responded to the infant's emotional displays. The dutiful response had in it an element of impatient "I don't know what's the matter with the child". My deduction was that in order to understand what the child wanted the mother should have treated the infant's cry as more than a demand for her presence. From the infant's point of view she should have taken into her, and thus experienced, the fear that the child was dying. It was this fear that the child could not contain. He strove to split it off together with the part of the personality in which it lay and project it into the mother. An understanding mother is able to experience the feeling of dread, that this baby was striving to deal with by projective identification, and yet retain a balanced outlook. [Bion, 1959, p. 104]

It seems to me that one can distinguish a moment in which, while splitting off and projecting the fear and a corresponding part of the self, the *state of mind in the infant remains dominated by the infantile distress* and not by the omnipotence of projective identification. Colman has talked in terms of the "gesture" of the infant and the mother's sensitive recognition and response to it. While this is appealing and no doubt correct, it seems incomplete in that it does not take account of the attempt to split off and project something into the mother. What seems critical to me is state of mind and, in particular, the "sense of identity" at any given moment. Of course with very young infants it is perhaps problematic to speak of a sense of identity. However, there can be little doubt that this quickly recedes as the infant matures. Certainly when we talk about infantile states of mind in an adult, I believe the distinction can be made with some confidence.

Can we then distinguish between a kind of infantile sense of identity—accompanied by a splitting-off and projecting of feelings, parts of the self, and of linked internal objects—and a narcissistic sense of identity characterized by an arrogant certainty—both using projection but to very different ends? The first would be something closer to "projective identification" in Bion's sense, a container/contained relationship as a primitive form of non-verbal communication. The second would be a sense of identity characteristic of intrusive identification in which any linking essential for communication is attacked and perverted. Of course, this distinction, while useful for our analysis of different states of mind, is at the same time difficult to sustain in the consulting-room, where the complexity of the phenomena means that one state oscillates with the other almost imperceptibly.

I raise this issue because it seems to me that the container/contained relationship is an important aspect of the intimacy of the adult couple. That is, it is possible that one partner is in an infantile state of mind, for example in distress and panic, while the other partner can be in a very different state of mind from that of projective identification with a parenting figure. It can be, as I described with Mr and Mrs R, that the "parent–child" relationship between them could be experienced as much a humiliation for the one, as it was an experience of superiority for the other. But just as the mother might relate to her infant in distress, receiving those projections, the partner might in a similar way act as a "container". We might say that the mother "identifies" with her distressed infant because she has access to her own infantile parts of the self, while at the same time not being overwhelmed either by the projections or by her own infantile anxieties. This could be possible when she is in introjective identification with an internal containing object— ultimately, the internal parental couple. It is what I am calling the "adult sense of identity". This kind of "parent–child" relationship was one Mr and Mrs R seldom, if ever, experienced.

Although the infant in that instance could be said to be projecting parts of the self, it does not seem to me that the infant is necessarily in the state of mind we have described as characteristic of *intrusive* projective identification. Similarly, the partner may be in distress but not in that "intrusive projective identification state of mind". As with the infant, this is no doubt possible only when relating to the partner who is in an "adult state of mind" in introjective identification with the internal parental couple. They share the same "internal geography" and the same "emotive world" by virtue of their shared infantile identification. What is added is that the adult partner can sustain that infantile identification *and* the introjective identification with the internal containing object *at the same time*.

Here I think we must leave this conundrum. "Projective identification" remains a term used in different ways in the psychoanalytic literature. What I think is important is that we keep in mind the distinction between infantile identification and narcissistic identification, especially when we are trying to understand the couple relationship. It will help to turn now to the third kind of identification—introjective identification, and the possibility of an adult sense of identity.

Introjective identification and intimacy

When we talk about an adult or an adult part of the self, we usually have in mind some undefined, or perhaps undefinable, sense of being "grown up" in emotional as well as physical terms. If pressed to define it more precisely, we might turn to our understanding of maturational processes, although we are faced with the dilemma that there is no obvious correlate to the genetic coding that contains a "blueprint", so to speak, of what the organism can and will become under optimal circumstances—for example, the acorn matures into the full-grown oak tree. Meltzer offers a view of the development of the adult part of the self and of the adult sense of identity in terms of the relationship with one's internal objects and in particular as a function of introjective identification.

Again here, as with the projective form or intrusive form of narcissistic identification, I want to distinguish between the "dynamics" of the identificatory process and the "phenomenology" of the state of mind attendant on introjective identification. The latter is critical for understanding the nature of the internal objects as well as the qualities of the sense of self vis-à-vis these internal objects. There is an essential reciprocity between these two aspects of the identification.

When Meltzer links "introjective identification" with the development of the "adult part of the self", it is important to note that he is talking about a very specific kind of introjective identification—that is, identification with a very particular kind of object. In order to think about this object—the "combined object" or the internal-parental-couple-in-coitus—we can do no better than to turn to Britton's lucid account of the Oedipal drama building on the insights of Melanie Klein into the link between Oedipus complex and the depressive position (Britton, 1989). I have discussed the work of Britton, Feldman, and O'Shaughnessy on this topic elsewhere (Fisher, 1993), and I do not want to rehearse it here. What I do want to suggest is how the development of what Britton has called "triangular space" is linked with the state of mind Meltzer associates with introjective identification with the internal combined object.

Britton suggests that initially the parental link is conceived in primitive part-object terms. If the link between the parents perceived in love and hate can be tolerated in the child's mind, it provides a prototype for an object relationship of a third kind, in which he is a witness and not a participant. Given this, it is possible to envisage both observing and being observed, which in turn creates a sense of space outside the self and within the self. This internal "triangular space" is also the basis for the adult part of the self and the adult sense of identity.

> It includes, therefore, the possibility of being a participant in a relationship and observed by a third person as well as being an observer of a relationship between two people. . . . The capacity to envisage a benign parental relationship influences the development of a space outside the self capable of being observed and thought about, which provides the basis for a belief in a secure and stable world. [Britton, 1989, 86–87]

It will be seen that this development provides the internal setting in which introjective identification with the creative parental couple becomes the core of what Meltzer calls the identification with the superego–ideal. It also leads to a state of mind characteristic of the depressive position. The phenomenology of this state of mind is familiar.

> Commitment to this identification rests upon the emotions of the depressive position, especially gratitude and the desire for worthiness. For this reason elements of the experience of sense-of-identity that relate to introjective identification have a prospective quality, an aspirational tone that is quite different from the immediate and delusional self-feeling produced by projective identification. Tentativeness, humility, self-doubt, and like nuances of emotion therefore attach to these aspects of the sense of identity and make up the shadings of a person's character that most impress us as sincere. [Meltzer, 1971/1994, p. 205]

There are moments in long analytic therapy with couples gridlocked in their claustrum world when we get a glimpse of the possibility of such a state of mind. The reader may be disappointed that I have not attempted to give a clinical illustration of introjective identification with the combined object or mature parental couple. Like the mastering of the anxieties of the depressive position, it is a state of mind to which we and our patients aspire, but which is easier to illustrate by the failure to achieve it. I do not mean, however, that it is unfamiliar. The mother responding to the projections of her baby, able to identify with the infant's experience because she has access to her own infantile anxieties, may also be able to "contain" the baby's projections in Bion's sense. She can do so *because she is in introjective identification with a containing internal object, the internal parental couple.*

It is a state of mind, a sense of identity that we as therapists seek to sustain in our analytic encounter with couples. And yet we know well how difficult that is to do when confronted with a claustrum that draws us into countertransference acting-in of a particular kind. What lies at the heart of this experience is what Feldman has described as the patient's struggle with an internal Oedipal couple engaged in some bizarre and often violent interaction, "a parental figure or couple that he finds impenetrable, unable to receive or respond to his projections". This, in turn, gives rise to violent attempts to get through or a sense of a hopeless situation that cannot be faced (Feldman, 1989, p. 126–127).

O'Shaughnessy has more recently described this kind of internal couple as a "remnant couple"—a remnant of the Oedipal couple that aroused so much emotion and anxiety that it was a signal to the psyche to obliterate it. These remnant couples are, depending on the nature and extent of the attack on them, sterile, voyeuristic and exhibitionistic, or sadomasochistic (O'Shaughnessy, 1993). Clinically, these internal "remnant couples" are of fundamental importance because identification with them lies at the heart of the dilemma of many of the couples who come to therapy, especially the gridlocked couples imprisoned in their claustrum world. In her paper O'Shaughnessy describes three individuals with different kinds of internal "remnant couples" who are similar in many ways to the three individuals Di Ceglie describes (chapter three).

The description of these individual patients and the kind of relationships they have with their analyst is familiar to therapists who work with couples. However, we do not always catch sight of the picture of these internal "remnants" of the creative parental couple in the frantic and often vicious acting-in that characterizes most sessions. What we catch sight of are the "traces" of these internal "remnant couples" enacted in the session with us. Mr and Mrs P were unusual in the glimpses of their internal worlds that they gave us through their dreams. This opaqueness of acting-in with which we most often struggle is one reason why awareness of the descriptive phenomenology of projective identification is so important for therapists who work with couples. I would like to conclude with one final dream recounted by Mrs P in the session following Mr P's "hypodermic" dream—evidence of an unconscious phantasy that helped to make sense of their shared difficulty in emotional intimacy with each other and with us. It was a dream, I suggest, of an internal "remnant couple" that precluded any possibility of identification with a creative parental couple. In a sense it formed one of the "templates" for the relationship between Mr and Mrs P, to use O'Shaughnessy's term.

Mrs P told of a dream:

> She was in a beautiful garden. She described vividly the weaving of flowers strung on cotton thread that formed a backdrop, realizing later in the dream that they signified a wedding. She saw her brother coming towards her wearing her dressing-gown. As he got closer, she realized he was larger on top, sort of a strange shape, as if he were developing breasts. Slowly it dawned on her that he had had a sex change and had become a woman. He told her he was getting married.

Later in the session she said she thought he was marrying a friend of his, to whom she knew he was close. Then she told us she had had another dream:

> She saw her father's chair on the veranda—the long-dead father she often had told us had wished she had been a son, although she was the competent one, while her brother was a miserable, weak failure. She either grabbed hold of the chair or of her father, she couldn't tell which, saying she missed him.

Here we get a glimpse of a transsexual or transvestite or homosexual internal couple whose dominant characteristic was confusion. There was evidence here of a longing for a father who could accept her as she was, mirroring perhaps her inability to tolerate the reality of the parental couple. But she could never be sure whether she could get hold of him or of an empty sign of his absence. Instead, what we see is a "remnant couple", a "combined object" of a perverse kind. Identification with this internal couple could only mean a sense of identity marked by confusions, a delusion of identity, and, for the couple, a delusion of intimacy.

In contrast, a state of mind marked by the concern for the object—and in the couple, concern for the other—includes capacity for appreciation and gratitude at being treated by the other in terms of needs. We are describing the intimacy possible within the depressive position. It is a state of mind marked by humility in the face of the infinitely unknowable mystery of the reality of the other. It makes possible a *reciprocity* in the experience of intimacy. It includes the emotional intensity of the spontaneity of the infantile parts of the personality but has the capacity to weather the turbulence and fleeting quality of the infantile life. And it is very different in tone and depth of emotion from the part-object "use" of the other in narcissistic relating.

In my paper on the claustrum, I wrote:

One of the most important points I wish to make in this paper is to highlight the fundamental difference between a genuine intimacy with the other and a "pseudo-intimacy" which is a narcissistic form of relating. The former is based on the reality that the other is known *only* from the outside. The latter is based on the phantasy of getting *inside* the other. Meltzer invites us to consider the difference between the picture of the inside of the internal mother which results from the use of *imagination* and the one which results from the phantasy of omnipotent intrusion. The imaginative "knowing" of the other, inspired by an imaginative "knowing" of the internal mother, is constructed necessarily out of elements of experience of the external world, respecting the privacy of the interior of the mother. It is characterised by an attitude which Bion has brought into our vocabulary from

his reading of John Keats. Keats described this attitude of
mind as *negative capability*, "that is, when [one] is capable of
being in uncertainties, mysteries, doubts, without any irrita-
ble reaching after fact and reason" [Bion, 1970, p. 125]. No
matter how intimate the "knowledge" of the other, it is always
characterised by uncertainties, mysteries and doubts.
[Fisher, 1993, pp. 10–11]

Such a state of mind is a pre-condition for mature object relating
and thus of intimacy in the most profound sense in the adult
couple.

PART TWO

CHAPTER SIX

Donald Meltzer in discussion

with James Fisher

A s we talked about how I might introduce him to the readers of this book—many of whom will need no introduction—Dr Meltzer spoke about the autobiographical stories in Isaac Bashevis Singer's *In My Father's Court* (1979). The "court" in Singer's book, or *Beth Din* in the Yiddish in which these stories were originally written, is the rabbinical court, an ancient institution among the Jews. In his introductory note, Singer wrote:

> The Beth Din was a kind of blend of a court of law, synagogue, house of study, and, if you will, psychoanalyst's office where people of troubled spirit could come to unburden themselves. That such a mixture was not only feasible but necessary was proved by the continued existence of the Beth Din over many generations. ... The Beth Din could exist only among a people with a deep faith and humility, and it reached its apex among Jews when they were completely bereft of worldly power and influence. [Singer, 1979]

It reminded me of a story Dr Meltzer told, at the book launch for *Sincerity and Other Works* (1994). He told about giving his graduation speech from memory at his high-school graduation. When, in the middle of it, he went completely blank, he heard the audience his father's "lovely, friendly laugh". He thought to himself that his father was thinking that he himself would not even have been able to get up and try to make such a speech. At that moment, his memory came back, and he carried on. Had you heard the story that day, you would have been in no doubt that this was not a "laughing *at* him". Instead of the "internal mob—whispering and raising their eyebrows", which Dr Meltzer says plagues him as a writer, this is a story both about the memory of his father *and* the presence of an internal object that is alive for him and came alive for those in the audience that day.

One thing I regret about this edited transcript collated from four "interviews" with Dr Meltzer is that it is impossible to convey his own gentle laugh, which accompanied many of his observations. Those who have heard him speak will know what I mean. His suggestion at the end of the discussion that the psychoanalyst shares his internal objects with his patient is a thought that paints a remarkable picture of the intimacy of the analytic relationship, as well as of the dependence at the heart of human experience. It is true not just of the analyst, but of the teacher, the parent, and indeed, any partner in an intimate relationship.

In this discussion with Dr Meltzer, the reader has an opportunity to "listen" to him in the presence, I believe, of the "lovely, friendly laugh" of his father—as well as, he tells us, his analyst and teacher, Melanie Klein, and teachers, colleagues, and friends, Roger Money-Kyrle, Esther Bick, Wilfred Bion, Martha Harris, among others.

It is true that for the diligent student of his work, Dr Meltzer has not added significantly in this discussion to what he has already said in his numerous publications. For most readers, however, it may be a pointer to things with which they are not familiar. In fact, it may be frustrating to those largely unfamiliar with his work in that it moves from topic to topic without the systematic exposition that might make his remarks more accessible.

Readers will also have to cope with the fact that my muddles, questions, and preoccupations will not be theirs, and, therefore,

I sometimes steer the discussion in directions they would not have chosen. To some extent, it represents my struggles with Dr Meltzer's thinking, and this may be helpful at times and distracting at others. I have included some references when I thought they might offer the reader somewhere to seek clarification.

I am not clear to what extent it is recognized that Dr Meltzer is a rigorously systematic thinker. That may not be obvious to those who dip occasionally into his, by now substantial, corpus of published papers and books. He himself once described his writings as "rather rambling", like Alpine villages "each positioned according to the rocks beneath", and "only loosely, and in a sense jaggedly, interconnected" (Meltzer, 1986, p. 9). We are indebted to Dr Alberto Hahn for the editing and publication of Dr Meltzer's collected papers, some of which had not been published previously and others were published in places that are not easily accessible (Meltzer, 1994). Taken together, Dr Meltzer's writings constitute what is a remarkably systematic "metapsychology", building especially on the work of Melanie Klein and W. R. Bion.

Readers who are interested in this metapsychology will find in this discussion with Dr Meltzer some ideas that may prompt them to explore further. Others, I think, will just relax and enjoy the friendly and generous way in which Dr Meltzer talks about what interests him. For those of us who struggle to work in a psychoanalytic way with couples, we may find ourselves occasionally challenged, sometimes amused, and even at times bewildered. But mainly, I believe, readers will find this discussion, and Dr Meltzer himself, alive in a way that exemplifies the content of his thinking—alive, that is, to the reality of the internal world and the internal objects on whom we are ultimately dependent. It is an invitation into "his father's court".

JAMES FISHER: In *The Claustrum* [Meltzer, 1992], you describe discovering for yourself that when Mrs Klein was talking about projective identification, she had in mind, it seemed, external objects, and you were beginning to make sense of projective identification with internal objects.

DONALD MELTZER: I think, judging by the original paper [on projective identification: Klein, 1946] and also the paper on identification [Klein, 1955] that Mrs Klein really had in mind the evolution of a state of mind *consequent* to projective identification. Although she wrote about it as if it were primarily with an object of envy and admiration as an external object, it didn't seem really from either paper that there was much relationship externally with that object— that it was really in phantasy and could be construed really as with internal objects. I think she was not absolutely clear in her own mind about the issue of "internal" and "external".

JF: How much difference does that distinction make?

DM: It makes a difference, particularly when you are talking about couples and when you are talking about the operation of projective identification in intimate relationships. Then it makes a very big difference. I think one of the reasons is that there is also a phenomenon that has a very strong resemblance to it that is really mutual projective identification in action, and it seems to give rise to what we call a *folie-à-deux* relationship. In the case of couples, it can give rise to sadomasochism, which is probably its most frequent phenomenology. But it can also give rise to what is

---

Note: this edited transcript was based on four tape-recorded interviews with Dr Meltzer in Oxford on November 24, December 8, and December 15, 1994, and on February 23, 1995.

sometimes called the "doll's-house" marriage, in which people seem to behave as if they were fused in their heads and think and speak in terms of the couple using the pronoun "we" instead of "I", for instance. They not only seem to be in harmony, they seem really to have identical points of view and identical values and identical experiences and so on. This form of fusion by projective identification seems to be different from the schizoid mechanism that Mrs Klein was talking about. It seems to be really a rather sophisticated mechanism and much more closely connected with hysterical and obsessional phenomena than with schizoid mechanisms, as far as I can tell.

JF: I can see that this would indeed seem to result in a *folie à deux*, but the idea that this is different from what Mrs Klein had in mind with the notion of projective identification invites us, I think, to rethink the notion of "mutual projective identification". But what would you say, jumping to the other end of the spectrum, about any of those mechanisms or defences operating in a so-called "normal" couple relationship where there may be moments of something going on between the partners that might look like that?

DM: This probably brings up the difference between moments of *con*-fusion and moments of fusion. Speaking in terms of moments, and the dynamics of a particular moment, is different from viewing the relationship as being in some continuous way characterized by a particular mental operation between the two people. I am sure that these moments of fusion and confusion happen in every couple.

JF: So it might be a sign of mental health that people can manage those moments—that is, they can move in and out of those momentary modes of relating.

DM: Yes, it bears on the difference between *being* confused and *feeling* confused. Where it is momentary—states of being confused—people recover from it and feel confused and then work it out by communication. This would seem to be the normal healthy process between couples: the moments of confusion, followed by feeling confused and then working it out by communication.

JF: It is perhaps the point for which some people are using the concept of "projective identification" in Bion's sense and talk about some form of non-verbal communication.

DM: Non-verbal communication, yes. I would not think it comes under that, although the movement from feeling confused to communication can certainly pass through communication by projective identification in Bion's sense, in a non-intrusive, non-coercive sense. But I would not want to confuse the two or see them as equivalent to one another. They involve a very different "mental motion", you might say, towards the other person. Projective identification in the Kleinian sense is really quite aggressive and intends to control and manipulate the mental state of the other person. When it is mutual, it amounts to a fencing duel—even open warfare, control and dominance, and so on. It's quite aggressive.

JF: In the sadomasochistic couple, they seem to be satisfied or even pleased with this in some peculiar way.

DM: Yes, in the sadomasochistic couple of course they settle into enacting a projective identification phantasy, and the driving force of it, it seems to me, is always discovered to be an intrusion into the parental intercourse and the murdering of the prospective baby. And it is a collusive relationship.

JF: Are you using "sadomasochistic" in a broad sense, or would you say that there are other forms of those kinds of collusive relationships?

DM: I think collusion is a mode of relationship and may or may not involve projective identification, and may or may not involve sadomasochism. It is a particular mode of alliance that is not the same as friendship or intimacy. It is really an alliance for a shared aim. It is essentially a political relationship.

JF: Thinking about Mrs Klein's papers on schizoid mechanisms [Klein, 1946] and on identification [Klein, 1955], and then considering Bion's paper on attacks on linking [Bion, 1959], where he develops Mrs Klein's notion of projective identification, it seems to me to make a huge leap in his picture of the communicative function of projective identification, almost describing a different phenomenon from that which Mrs Klein had been describing.

DM: Well, one is accustomed in Mrs Klein to see, in the paranoid–schizoid position, attacks on thought, but not attacks on thinking. That, it seems to me, is a great leap forward. Bion envisages attacks on functions and not just on the products of functions. Mrs Klein is concerned with unconscious phantasy and thinking and the relationships that embody them and so on. Bion has moved things forward in a huge leap into the depths in [the notion of] attacks on functions themselves.

JF: But in a sense it is hard to see projective identification as anything other than an attack on thinking, and yet for him it is an act of communication.

DM: Well, that is a different kind of "projective identification"— that is the non-intrusive projective identification for the sake of non-verbal communication.

JF: If you go from Mrs Klein's paper to Bion's paper, one struggles to see how they could be talking about the same thing, although he calls it "projective identification".

DM: Well, I think he has probably made more a tactical than a theoretical error.

JF: When you make the distinction between "intrusive" identification, meaning what Mrs Klein called "projective identification", and projective identification in Bion's sense of a communicative interaction [see, for example, Meltzer, 1986, pp. 66–69], is that a distinction that, if Bion were here, he would say, "yes, of course"—or is that an unfair question?

DM: You are asking me whether I think Bion would understand me. I would say, no better than I understand him. We have very different mentalities.

JF: I recognize that this sort of hypothetical question cannot really be answered. What I am trying to ask is whether it was a distinction developed in thinking and working with Bion, or whether you were standing back from what Bion has said, saying, "well, it must be that we have two different notions here".

DM: Well, I hardly ever worked with Bion. I had no supervisions with him, I had only seminars with him. I can never say I worked with Bion. It is only really his writings that I know, and that, of course, is very problematic, to say the least.

JF: But is there any connection between the two? This distinction that you make between "intrusive" identification in Mrs Klein's sense and "projective" identification in Bion's sense seems very helpful, although many people seem to ignore it.

DM: Well, Bion's description of projective identification for the communication of thought certainly lacks the concreteness of splitting and projective identification involved in Mrs Klein's intrusive identification. It's all about functions and the content of these functions.

JF: Mrs Klein specifically talks about urethral and excretory functions—of projecting those, of putting those into the mother. Elizabeth Bott Spillius [see Spillius, 1988a] says that Kleinian analysts today would interpret less in terms of anatomical structures such as breast or penis and more in terms of psychological functions such as seeing, hearing, thinking, evacuating. Might there be some link between this and the distinction between Bion's "projective identification" and Mrs Klein's intrusive identification?

DM: I think that Mrs Klein's concept of splitting and projective identification always implies a cognitive part of the self. To my mind it involves a very *concrete* intrusion inside the object, and this cognitive aspect bifurcates into the identificatory and the projective or claustrophobic aspects of being inside.

JF: When you speak of the projective or claustrophobic aspect, you mean a cognitive aspect of the self that could be aware or make judgements or have perceptions—what might be thought of as having "experiences"—*inside* the object.

DM: It lives in there, and it lives in there as a particular world. This world has a particular organization and particular qualities. And although in many ways it has resemblances and derives its forms from the outside world, its ethos is its own. It is essentially very primitive.

JF: The difference, then, between these projective or claustrophobic aspects and the identificatory aspects includes the idea that the latter have to do with the nature of the self itself?

DM: Yes, and the nature of the self of the object with which an immediate identification tends to take place—that is, the self of the object as conceived, as imagined by the self of the intruder.

JF: Does that always happen? Is it a common feature that the identification is not just an intrusion, but an identification *with* the object into which the intrusion has been made?

DM: That is my impression. As soon as a part of the self enters or intrudes into the object phenomenologically, there is this simultaneous bifurcation in its experience. It does not involve a splitting but is something that happens simultaneously. It experiences *both* this identification *and* the claustrophobic qualities of this world.

JF: Is that why Mrs Klein used the term projective *identification*, then—she had in mind this process of identification with the object?

DM: She had in mind *only* the idea of projective identification with the object. It was, I think, to her mind the discovery of the mechanism of narcissistic identification.

JF: You distinguish these claustrophobic experiences into three broad areas [Meltzer, 1992]. But it could be said that some seem more claustrophobic than others?

DM: Oh, yes. Projective identification into the breast is positively *claustrophilic*. Even the genital projection is rather claustrophilic and gives rise to a kind of erotomania. The projective identification into the breast gives rise to a "lotus-eater's" kind of mentality.

JF: In our work with couples, insofar as we encounter intrusive identification, primarily we must be encountering the intrusion into the rectum [see Fisher, 1994].

DM: I think it is probably primarily intrusion into the rectum, because what brings these couples is that largely they are dogged by sadomasochism.

JF: Sometimes these couples might report a phase of their relationship that was highly eroticized, although this is not the state they are in at the moment.

DM: Yes, it may have started really in this lotus eater's kind of blissfulness and indolence and so on. The honeymoon is often of that quality. What I described in *The Claustrum* [Meltzer, 1992] is this definite helter-skelter tendency for the phenomenology to descend through the genital into the rectum.

JF: That would help us to understand some couples. I am thinking of one in particular, where they describe this Nirvana-like experience that they had at the beginning, and which they can occasionally achieve when they go off away from the children and have this ecstatic experience with each other. We thought of it as a fusion, but it might be thought of as this kind of erotomania of intrusion in unconscious phantasy into the mother's genital [see Fisher, 1994].

DM: I think the sense of fusion is indigenous to all the phenomenology of projective identification—the loss of boundaries of self, the illusion of extraordinary intimacy, and so on.

JF: So you think that it accounts for the extraordinary disappointment or the intensity of the relationship when they come asking for therapy, because they have that counterbalancing experience of something that was almost unreal in its excitement?

DM: Yes.

JF: One of the most puzzling ideas, I think, for most of us to think about is the projective identification with internal objects. Thinking about the relationship between the couple and the relationship that is going on in their internal world with internal objects, sometimes we talk about that as an externalization of the internal object. How would you see the interpersonal aspect of this fit in with the notion of projective identification into the internal object?

DM: In the case of the couple, each of them identifies the other as an aspect of the internal object. For example, the man may experience the woman as the sadistic mother, the imprisoning mother, the erotic mother, the protective mother. It is all part of the breaking-out of childhood into what is thought to be the adult world.

JF: That always has a pseudo-quality in these relationships, this adult quality is always . . .

DM: It has pseudo-mature quality, yes. It is usually pompous or pretentious or fragile and so on.

JF: I was struck with one couple, where, when they had a child, each of them could relate to the baby in what felt like a more mature way, but when they related to each other, it reverted back to this very infantile relationship. Why is it that they managed it with the baby? Why is it that he can tolerate the baby with her outbursts and her moods, and be quite gentle but firm with her, but when his wife is ill, he can sometimes become so unreasonable. He was outraged, for example, when he rang and she did not answer because she was not well.

DM: Of course, the thing that makes it so difficult for the thera-pist to follow is the patient who is continually "in and out". It is not just a change in mood, it is a change in perception of the world. Whereas at one moment his own child may be experienced as a part-object, part of the mother, or part of the father, the next moment it is his child and he is con-cerned about her, feels tenderly towards her, and so on— and is not in projective identification. It is instability writ large when the person is in and out of projective identifica-tion. Of course you can see that represented in dreams where the patient is going from the outside to the inside and back again, and you see these changes in the percep-tion of the world.

JF: You emphasize and have explained that mother takes prior-ity in this process, that the question of some kind of projec-tive identification with the father is in a way secondary, or by means of access to mother, or in relationship to mother. Have I understood that—the role of the father here seems inherently secondary?

DM: So it seems to me—not only inherently secondary, but essentially part-object.

JF: At what point does that change with the role of the father? I am thinking of Oedipal dynamics appearing in the relationship.

DM: Again it is quite unstable. When a boy intrudes into the relationship between Mummy and Daddy, he immediately seems to relate to the father as a part-object.

JF: Psychoanalysis is a relationship of a couple—the patient and the analyst. I am still puzzled about the privacy of that kind of relationship, that is, attempting to think about the infantile transference to the analyst or therapist, that intimate relationship in the presence of the partner—or, alternatively, talking about the intimate relationship between the partners in the presence of the therapist. I know you do not see couples as such yourself.

DM: No, not really.

JF: What I was wondering—some of us feel puzzled about moving from the individual setting, where there is a kind of intimate relationship, and getting involved with a couple, where there is an intimate relationship in the presence of the other, or a sense of looking at their intimate relationship and at the relationship that develops with you as a therapist.

DM: Well, I think that with the kind of people who seek couple therapy, it seems to me they come with a very rich preformed transference—that is, as a couple seeking parental guidance and support and discipline and so on. They come with an infantile pre-formed transference as a couple.

JF: Can you say more about this notion of a "pre-formed" transference?

DM: When you think about the beginning of psychoanalysis, when the patients knew nothing about psychoanalysis, it might not have been such a distinctive phenomenon. But at present very few patients come to analysis without having ideas about it, and what it is going to be, and what it should be, and what it is not, and so on. All of that, and the behaviour that reflects it, constitutes a pre-formed transference that really has to be dismantled before there is room enough, as it were, for a genuine transference response—before the actual performance and process and mentality of the analyst can be allowed to make its individual impact. And, of course, every analysis, for that reason, is somewhat different and is related to what Freud called the "particularities" of the analyst—of his mentality as well as his physical particularities. But when the patient comes originally, he has a professional pre-formed transference, usually full of ideas and full of expectations and full of limitations and doubts and misgivings and so on. It is the sort of thing that also prevents people from falling in love—that they have pre-formed ideas about the opposite sex, for instance—and this leaves very little possibility for abandoning themselves to the experience of falling in love. On the other hand, there are patients who come and promptly fall in love in the transference, and this is where you can see this really infantile process of the aesthetic impact and the flight from it.

JF: You are suggesting, then, that the couple would come with a particular kind of pre-formed transference, not so much to psychoanalysis or what they understand of an analytic relationship, but more to a parental figure for guidance?

DM: Yes, I think that the people who come for couple therapy are probably involved with one another in a very infantile way and need parental guidance as a pre-formed transference. They are not seeking investigation but are coming to be instructed, or chastised, or told to love one another, and so on.

JF: That raises the question of the expectation of what is on offer for somebody coming for therapy. Someone might question offering a kind of analytic opportunity to someone who comes with that sort of expectation, wanting things sorted out, wanting problems sorted out.

DM: So long as you do not misrepresent the product that you are offering, the patient's expectations are no more valid than those of any other purchaser of any item. So long as he does not say, "I want some sterling silver", and you say, "I have some lovely sterling silver. I know it does not look like sterling silver, but it really is." I mean, that's fraud, and if you accommodate yourself to the patient's expectations, that's a kind of fraud or seduction.

JF: But it does raise the question of the old issue about what is analysis for. Previously, people came with some symptom, while these days people come to analysis more because of long-standing difficulties, and in some sense they have an idea what they want to understand—they want analysis in some way.

DM: Yes, well, I think generally analysts these days make it clear to their patients fairly early that they do not analyse symptoms away, that analysis is an investigation, and since it is largely an investigation into people's muddles and confusions, it is expected that if it clarifies things, it will do them good in some way. But analysts make no specific promises, and if patients find that they don't like it, they should feel free to leave, and do. What the analyst does do—which I think is legitimate—is to encourage patients to continue when they are feeling discouraged, and they are usually discouraged because they are no better.

JF: I had a couple yesterday where the man was complaining that it was costing a lot of money and a lot of time, a hundred times the cost of a "do-it-yourself" book, and he was not getting the advice he needed.

DM: Yes—I'd say to him, you've come to the wrong place, of course, if it is advice you want. That is not the business I am in.

JF: One of our assumptions at the Tavistock Marital Studies Institute is that one can use psychoanalytic concepts to understand the couple relationship in the same way that one understands the patient–analyst relationship in analysis.

DM: Yes, the most important thing is that you bring to bear psychoanalytic observations and you share your observations with the patient. I do not think concepts are very important, except in so far as concepts enable you also to observe things that you would not observe otherwise.

JF: One question is the field of observation. There is a debate about whether the observations should be limited to the couple relationship that you have in the room with you, as they describe it and as you see it, or whether that observation includes the relationship between the couple and the therapist. It is a debate about the transference and what gets interpreted.

DM: Everything that is visible in the room is available for interpretation, and by interpretation, of course, I mean mainly description. The interpretation of meaning is so implicit in the description that it really is not a separate matter. I think that went out with the concept of specific mechanisms of defence.

JF: The task of this observation, if I understand what you have said and written, is to facilitate the emergence of the infantile aspects of the personality—to clarify them, to name them, to make them available in some way to be thought about.

DM: I think so, yes, and in the hope of diminishing confusion—all sorts of confusions, in which things are either equated or are so split so apart as to seem to have no contact with one another. There are these two opposite types of confusion: confusion by lack of differentiation, confusion by splitting.

JF: This is a very different state of mind and a very different view of interpretation from that which intends to explain something to the patient or the couple—why this or how that.

DM: *How* is a different question from *why*. When you show a person how, you are showing them the sequence of events and how they lead into one another. You are not implying anything causal, and I think we are not dealing with causality really, we are dealing with judgements and decisions and values and so on.

JF: That would take us out of this interview and into another one—this question about causality.

DM: Yes, and it would lead into another direction to the educational function of analysis, which tends to be strongly denied, but, of course, the patients would not deny it.

JF: In one of the papers on interpretation, "On Routine and Inspired Interpretations" [Meltzer, 1973], you talk about a move from a pedagogical to a comradely relationship, some sense of joint exploration. Is that view of the psychoanalytic process commonly shared, do you think?

DM: I don't think so, no.

JF: This follows from some of the things in the tradition from Mrs Klein that people like Money-Kyrle have emphasized.

DM: The tradition in psychoanalysis is that interpretation is a form of instruction, as if that were something different from pedagogy. This left it in the position that it could be called "reductive".

JF: My impression is that working in a "standard" psychoanalytic way with couples has happened very little in the history of psychoanalysis. Do you have any thoughts about why that should be?

DM: I don't know. How does it operate at the Tavistock Marital Studies Institute?

JF: Well, what I think we are doing is trying to work and think in standard psychoanalytic ways, as we would with individual patients, but that seems to be a relatively rare thing, and not many people are doing that. It is very difficult to get psychoanalysts interested in analytic work with couples.

DM: Well, I think it is a more difficult challenge because you really have to get out of the grandstand and onto the field and still function as a referee.

JF: Is it, then, more like child analysis or child psychotherapy?

DM: It is more participating. I think that people have approached marital studies as commentators rather than as participants in a three-way scramble, or a four-way scramble. I would think that may be psychotherapeutic, but it is not psychoanalytic. It's hard to get into the middle of a couple, not only hard to avoid getting your shins kicked, but they can also be suspicious of your feelings and motives if you are at all either attracted or repelled by either of them.

JF: My impression is that some people would think that you

altered the analytic structure by inviting the couple into that experience. It would be seen as not analytic.

DM: Well, the partner is always there in an analysis, only the partner is not able to speak for himself or herself. And the analyst's problem is to discern the misrepresentations. I would not think it is very different when you are actually with a couple. You have your referee functions, but you have also your "throwing-in-the-ball" functions, as it were, to keep the game moving. I would not think it is all that different, but I can see that the technique of it has its own special stresses and difficulties. There are also counter-transference difficulties involved. But I would not think it departs from the types of difficulties of analytic practice, although how you can manage analysis in a group is just a mystery to me.

JF: What do you see as the primary difference?

DM: I cannot imagine my mind working fast enough to observe the individual metapsychology in operation. I feel as if I would, at best, just be picking up general atmospheres and things of that sort. But I have never done any group therapy since I was beginning in the field and found that I hated it then!

JF: Bion talks about a sort of group mind, doesn't he? There is a phenomenon of the group mental life peculiar to the group itself, almost as if there were a group state of mind.

DM: I think Bion was quite unique in his ability to gather a group together without any intention of benefiting—he would even mock them for expecting to be benefited. His model of the good officer who is afraid neither of the hatred nor of the love of his troops would not appeal to me as a model for therapy. I think it is very good, but it would not appeal to me at all.

JF: It seems to me that one of the important contributions you have made is the emphasis on interpretation as observation rather than explanation. Can you say a bit more about observation in the consulting-room?

DM: Psychoanalytically speaking, I have various masters from whom I have taken various things. From Mrs Klein I have taken interpretation. From Money-Kyrle I have taken patience and kindness. From Bion, thinking. But from Mrs Bick I took observation. She was a great observer—not just baby observation, but clinical observation. I think that it is not an easy thing to learn, because in our intellectual climate there is such an emphasis on words, and such a litigious emphasis on precise recollection of language—it is best on paper, to get it on paper and fix it, and so on. But the point about psychoanalytic observation of people's talking is that it has to do with the things that you cannot get on paper—not just the musical aspect of it, but the things in which listening and interpreting are so tied up together that it relates to the things that I have called, for instance, the "temperature" and "distance" of the communication, which are so important in the psychoanalytic situation— both to observe the temperature the patient is emanating and also to observe the temperature that you yourself are emanating and whether it is raising or lowering the temperature that the patient is emanating. And, as well, to observe this business about distance, because intimacy does require a certain closing of the distance of conversation, as you do automatically in just ordinary cocktail-party behaviour, as it were. The varying of the distance from the person that you are talking to carries this tremendous significance, that if you move an inch closer, a woman feels you are practically raping her, and things of that sort.

JF: That, of course, presents a challenge with a couple, because the distance you are with one partner has also a implication for the relationship with the other partner.

DM: It is more like volley-ball than it is like doubles in tennis for instance, because the ball gets bounced around on this side before it goes on to the other side of the court, and so on.

JF: What principle operates when you're thinking about distance? It seems to me you could say that we are now talking more about doing than observing. How does this relate to the observing?

DM: Observing the interplay of the different mental states.

JF: But you make a choice about where you psychologically position yourself.

DM: I am talking first about noticing where you have placed yourself. Then you can decide whether that is the right place to be.

JF: And then what principle operates about deciding what is the right place to be?

DM: Well, the principle that operates is the principle of the recognizing of the existence of this invisible barrier between the casual and the intimate. And it is a very rigid barrier; although it is invisible, it is discernible, and the ways in which you discern it are primarily through the counter-transference.

JF: And you can see that change in the course of the analytic process.

DM: Well, you see from the patient's dreams how much it changes. For example, you could see it in the dreams of one patient of mine, for whom the problem had always been that she rushed into intimacy and then quickly disappeared. The most recent dream was a dream in which *she woke up in the morning and realized that she was in a consulting-room in one bed, and I was in the consulting-room in another bed. And she thought to herself: "What's going on here?"* I interpreted this as meaning, "What *has* been going on here all these years?" She had been in analysis for about four years. And I said, what has been going on is a psycho-analytic love affair, which she conducted at the beginning, with a rush into sexual intimacy with me. I reminded her of the famous dream of the intercourse in the doorway: *as she was walking out of the consulting-room we suddenly had intercourse in the doorway.* Then, after that, for several years she kept disappearing, so I could make hardly any contact with her at all, until she gradually came back into the maternal transference, and this has begun gradually to develop a combined-object quality. She is a woman whose father was absent for six months at a time, working abroad, during most of her childhood, so his periodic returns were kind of explosive.

JF: She has a dream and says, "what's going on?"—and you say
     to her something like, "I think you mean, what has been
     going on?" That is an observation but it could also be seen
     as explaining something to her.

DM: Well, explaining to her what it meant in the dream that she
     had "been asleep"—and what that meant in terms of trans-
     ference relationship and it appearing only in her dreams in
     the course of these last few years of analysis.

JF: So the observation is almost, in a way, helping her to notice
     her own observation that she has "been asleep", to what is
     clear from the dreams—that what has been going on is a
     love affair.

DM: Yes.

JF: So in that sense you are inviting her to become an observer
     of her own experience.

DM: To notice—to notice the intensity of her feelings and the
     quality of her feelings in the transference.

JF: If we think about this concept of distance when there are
     two therapists in the consulting-room with a couple, there
     are two people wondering where we have placed our-
     selves—where I have placed myself, where my partner has
     placed herself. If you were in that situation, what would
     you be thinking about or noticing?

DM: Well, I would want to notice, first of all, which were the
     partnerships. They may not be the external-world partner-
     ships at all. It may be that you and one of the couple have
     become allied, and your partner is allied to the other. Then
     I would want to notice how much it is a game of skill and
     how much it is competition.

JF: In that sense it only widens the field, because there are
     more possibilities. The principle remains the same—ob-
     serving what is alive in the room.

DM: Yes, and putting a name to it.

JF: Can you say a bit more about temperature, or perhaps you
     can give an illustration of what you mean by the tempera-
     ture. Are you talking about the emotional intensity?

DM: The emotional intensity, that's right.

JF: You not only talk about observing the temperature but also about a kind of modulation.

DM: Modulation, yes—keeping the temperature at that moment at a workable level, which changes more or less systematically during the course of the analysis. The kind of temperature that sets patients running away in one session is the temperature that holds them in the intimacy in a later session.

JF: How would that be connected with regression? Some people talk about encouraging or not encouraging regression in the patient.

DM: Well, there is nothing that drives a schizophrenic into a regressed state like getting too warm with them. They really cannot tolerate it. It panics them, it confuses them.

JF: But do you aim to encourage a kind of manageable regression?

DM: No, I aim at discouraging any sort of regression by holding the patient in a workable contact.

JF: Could that be seen to be a prime difference of a Kleinian approach?

DM: I don't know if it is Kleinian. It is certainly my feeling that regression constitutes a loss of integration, and a loss of observation, and loss of a capacity to think, and so on. I can't see anything good about regression.

JF: I think people who would work that way would suggest that it's a kind of reworking process—that the patient gets regressed and relives through a process.

DM: That's a very Winnicottian view. I think it's dangerous and damaging. It generates omnipotence in the therapist and drives the patient wild.

JF: Encouraging the noticing, the observation: would you understand that in terms of a level of part of the self—that is, the more adult part of the self as the observer?

DM: No, I think the observation is connected with attention and is related to consciousness.

JF: Children are good observers, or can be.

DM: Can be. But generally it seems to me that in analysis one can assume that anything that is within the patient's sensory field is observed, but not necessarily paid attention to. The purpose of your comments as an analyst is to bring the patient's attention to notice the things that you yourself are noticing. A lot of the way in which you notice things, of course, is through, first of all, paying attention to your countertransference.

JF: It seems to me that this question of observation, the valuing of noticing, is also linked with the distinction you emphasize between thinking and doing, between communication and action. What you are interested in is communication?

DM: Yes, I'm interested in widening the field of attention and therefore enhancing the possibility of communication— Whereas any move towards action is really a move towards closing down.

JF: In terms of the transference, there is a question about using male and female co-therapists. The role of father and of the couple seems to be given more prominence.

DM: You complicate things because you not only introduce male and female concepts, you also introduce male and female *personalities* of a particular sort, one perhaps having more penetration than the other, or one having more attraction than the other, and it does skew the whole process.

JF: Do you think it obscures the process?

DM: Well, seeing a lone therapist, aside from the fact of being physically more male or more female, the flavour of the personality is not likely to be grossly different if it is a reasonably sane therapist, it seems to me. If you introduce two therapists, you have two very different personalities, along with their relationship to one another, which may or may not exist between them. It may exist only as a contractual relationship.

JF: Surely it exists as a professional relationship. But whether that is only a contractual relationship might be an interesting question—whether professional relationships in therapy are only contractual or whether they inevitably include something more than that.

DM: My impression is that professional relationships are contractual. And that intimate relationships are private and
are not on show in the consulting-room.

JF: I am still not clear how you think it skews it, then. That
sounds as if it might skew it in a way that would be
unrecoverable.

DM: It skews it in the same way that family life tends to be
matriarchal or patriarchal. It seems to be rather rare to find
families where there is this combined object balance—at
least, that is my impression.

JF: It might particularly be true because a lot of our co-therapy
partnerships are composed of a trainee and a senior therapist.

DM: Yes, it is even more likely to be true.

JF: What impact would that have on the analytic process, that
it is skewed by that imbalance, if there is an imbalance? Is
that not even more grist for the mill?

DM: Well, if it is an efficient miller, yes. That is generally true of
the analytic method. If the analyst is really efficient, he
makes use of everything. But if he is not so efficient, intru-
sions into the setting, for instance, raise hell.

JF: I am thinking of male and female co-therapists. It might be
one thing occasionally to introduce it to see what effect it
has, but as a practice, if it is skewing things in a way that is
unmanageable, we would want to review it, I think. One of
the arguments that was made by Henry Dicks [1967] at the
Tavistock Clinic was that he moved from two therapists to
one, with the suggestion that then the one therapist can
integrate all of the projections instead of having them split
between the two therapists. Is that similar to what you were
saying?

DM: Yes, I think two therapists is a kind of forlorn manipulative
experiment, and I would not really want to do it myself.

JF: "Forlorn" is rather a strong word. As is "manipulative".

DM: Well, I think it grows out of some sort of discouragement. I
think whenever you reach for technical modifications, it is
probably out of discouragement about understanding.

JF: Historically, it was because the couple were seen separately, each partner was seen separately, and then the Family Discussion Bureau [the early name of the Tavistock Marital Studies Institute], Dicks, and others experimented with being together in a foursome. It was actually seen as having quite a lot of advantages, rather than being a forlorn and manipulative experiment. But we are continually reviewing our way of working psychoanalytically with a couple. You see that as an alteration in the structure of the analytic relationship, but having the couple in a room as not. I have almost thought of it the other way round, that having the couple in the room raises questions about whether you can work psychoanalytically. You seem to be more positive about that and more negative about the two therapists.

DM: In the same way I am sceptical about group therapy. I think there is just too much going on for people to keep track of it all, either consciously or unconsciously—so that, I think, rather inevitably it simplifies itself into the basic assumption type of configuration. The one-to-one relationship in analysis seems to me to hover on the verge of being overwhelming. To follow the transference and countertransference—it is always on the verge of being too much for the individuals. It is difficult to see how multiplying the participants is likely to simplify it—quite the contrary.

JF: May I jump to something else, which we have not talked about? What I am wondering about in the couple relationship is this whole area of adhesive identification. At one point you describe a case of a child needing to have some object always around to provide a kind of second skin for integration. These objects were used almost as an exoskeleton. I am wondering about that in the couple relationship—whether sometimes we see that sort of desperation, a kind of adult adhesive identification.

DM: Adhesive identification is such an ordinary part of casual social contact that it is hard to assign it a pathological role, except where the development of dimensionality has been so set back that there is hardly any opportunity for anything but adhesive identification.

JF: I had not made that connection between contractual relationships and adhesive identification. If that is true, then most of our existence is characterized by some form of adhesive identification.

DM: Oh, I think it is such an ordinary part of what I call casual social contact. When you don't want to be bothered, adhesive identification is brought into play.

JF: Which is a way of saying that someone will identify with, for example, the association they might be part of. Their identity is shaped or formed by that link. Something like the army, for example: I am an officer in the army, and that is who I am. I identify with my regiment. Is that what you mean by adhesive identification in the adult?

DM: Yes, adhesive identification seems to consist of sort of sensually creeping around the surface of the other person in order to avoid any sort of mental stimulation. It is a bit like boxers in a clinch. It closes the distance in order to avoid contact—meaningful, communicative contact, or aggressive contact for that matter—mainly to avoid communication.

JF: One question that sometimes arises with regard to projective identification, insofar as it relates to an external object, is whether it involves introjective identification on the part of the other?

DM: My view is that communication is required for any sort of introjection and introjective identification. The danger in any sort of a group is that communication simply turns into the giving of orders and into actions, and thus communication becomes not feasible.

JF: Can you say more about the relationship between communication and introjective identification?

DM: I think that, except in the case of the other art forms, the transformation into language is such an essential part of the movement from part-objects to whole objects in the inner world.

JF: Language is at the heart of it?

DM: Well, that transformation is at the heart of it, of finding the language, the naming. Without that it remains as airy nothings, really.

JF: If it is *only* words, it is nothing. But if it is not put into words, then there is no possibility of memory, of thinking.

DM: Yes, I think it just remains as unconscious phantasy at part-object level and therefore plans for action. It does not constitute a relationship—communication is essential for a relationship.

JF: What is your view of other sorts of language? I am thinking of the Barenboim–duPres relationship, where, it was said, they could communicate with each other when they played together, she on the cello, he on the piano. There was a kind of communication, almost as if they were using the musical language in the way you were describing that transformation.

DM: Yes, the musical "language" is probably the great example of showing what becomes possible beyond the limits of language.

JF: So in a sense this transformation is not limited to language *per se*, but it is symbolic transformation—the transformation into symbol in some way.

DM: Yes, and symbols that can find either language or form or musical form.

JF: Psychoanalysis has sometimes been criticized for being so focused on words. But that is the reality of human experience, language being the transformation that makes us human.

DM: Well, I think it has been criticized for focusing on psychoanalytic words, which are rightly called jargon. We would not be criticized for being poetic. This what it needs to be. The great dreams, for example, are very simple and often poetic.

JF: How does one develop this capacity to listen, to be open to hearing the language of the patient?

DM: In trying to teach psychoanalysis to relative beginners, I find that the most difficult thing to get across is that you do not do analysis by listening, you do it by observation. And therefore to get a student to describe a session and not just give you a recording of the session, as it were, is very, very difficult, especially if they have not had an analytic experience of the sort where the analyst is continually describing his observations. It is necessary for the analyst to be able to draw the patient's attention to what is happening in his mind, not just to watch himself from the outside and notice his behaviour, his speech, and so on. In order to do that, the analyst has to be a really keen observer, and this is why this baby observation business is so important. Of course, the variation in the reports from baby observation students is as broad a spectrum as you can imagine. Some of them can really absolutely describe nothing, they can only behave like journalists and put down the facts, as it were.

JF: I suppose in terms of observation what we find difficult to do is to observe what is alive in the room.

DM: Yes, it is a field of observation. To listen is not listening like a recording machine. It is really listening to the language, listening to the music, listening for special uses of words that strike one as having symbolic references, and so on. Like a patient this morning—I can absolutely hear her hesitate over a certain word and tiptoe around it. She was describing how cold it was and how everything was touched with frost. She was about to say hoarfrost and could not bring herself. Then, of course, came a dream that showed quite clearly her mother accusing her of being a little whore.

JF: Somehow that brings to my mind your discussion of "falling in love" in *The Apprehension of Beauty* [Meltzer & Harris Williams, 1988], where you quote that lovely description from Robert Louis Stevenson. How do you understand "falling in love"?

DM: Well, it is a form of abandonment, first of all, which doesn't happen very often. It is a state of maximum hopefulness, as yet unqualified by observation and experience.

JF: Some people say that it has to be understood in broad terms as a kind of paranoid–schizoid state of mind and that working towards a more depressive position state of mind would not allow for this phenomenon of falling in love.

DM: Well, Freud thought it was an obsessional state. I think that is probably closer to it actually. Because in the abandonment of falling in love, the love object, and the hopes and aspirations towards it, do really swamp the mind and allow very little room for anything else, at least temporarily in the acute phase of falling in love. I think in a certain sense falling in love is always *at first sight*, even though it may not be in fact at first sight. It is the first sight of the object from a particular vertex, seeing it in a new light and so on.

JF: In *The Apprehension of Beauty* [Meltzer & Harris Williams, 1988] your model for that is the apprehension of the mother, of beauty of the mother, the breast, as the overwhelmingly beautiful object.

DM: That's right, an overwhelming sensual experience as yet very little qualified by experience and very little qualified by observation, just the impact.

JF: When one moves towards a depressive position state of mind, I can't help wondering whether there is another kind of experience that is possible when one is moving towards that end of the spectrum. Is there another kind, a second kind of falling in love?

DM: Well, I myself think of it in terms of the metaphor of the natural process of fertilization and ripening. In the case of fruits, of course, many are pollinated and few ripen. I have no idea what the factors are that determine this. But one can see it happening: they fertilize in clusters, and then, of the cluster, one or two ripen. Grapes are quite different. Grapes are fertilized and almost all ripen, with the exception of a few that remain tiny little green things. In nature there are different processes. I think the usual process amongst people of our culture who are capable of falling in love is that they fall in love many times before one ripens. In order to ripen, one can see that it requires a fairly high degree of reciprocity, as it does with the baby.

JF: And the relationship of that state of mind of the ripening of the relationship, the beauty of the object and that first sight of the beauty of the mother and the beauty of the breast, is this ripening a revisiting of that early experience?

DM: The initial impact of the object probably has its origins in quite ancient images and yearnings and expectations and tends to be fairly stereotypic. The ripening of it is ripening into the individuality of the love object. It departs from the stereotypic and becomes so highly individual as to be unique and irreplaceable and all of these things.

JF: The question of sincerity in your essay "Sincerity" [Meltzer, 1971/1994] is an interesting way to think about the question of intimacy and what it means. You link it with identification. Could you say a bit about the link between a sense of identity and the processes of identification?

DM: The sense of identity is a fluctuating item. It varies from context to context. For instance, when you are in a group, you have a different sense of identity and a different means by which you apprehend that sense of identity—that is, you imagine yourself in the audience observing yourself. Your sense of identity is what technically I think would be called an adhesive identity, because it is related to the surface, to your appearance, your gestures, the theatrical aspect of your performance in the context in which your performance is almost solely adaptational. It's very difficult to be in a group and to behave differently.

JF: Is it always linked with one's identifications? Is that how we come to our sense of identity?

DM: As soon as you move into the sphere that has any possibility of intimacy, then you move into the realm in which your sense of identity is achieved through various types of identification.

JF: So there is in fact a very close link between a sense of identity and identifications?

DM: Yes, the identifications in the situation in which there is any possibility of intimacy is apprehended by introspection and by recognizing the identificatory nature of your feelings and attitudes and so on. It has some depth to it. In so far as it's projective, of course, it makes the geographical mistake

of being identified with your object. This is where it becomes grandiose, and where it becomes touchy and claustrophobic and so on.

JF: Just for a moment can we look at what you call the "infantile sense of identity"? Is that state of mind the core of the
personality, that infantile sense of identity or identification?

DM: In so far as the infantile level apprehends the introjected
object as in relation to it, it is a family situation in which
you are one of the children. This you experience very much
in the analytic situation, where you experience it as externalized in the form of the transference.

JF: And this again is related to the introjected internal objects?

DM: That's right, and it's qualities are in relation to these
introjected objects and their qualities.

JF: This would be connected in some way with the perspective
that the core of the personality is relational—that is, that
you don't talk about a kind of impulse-defined self, a kind
of infantile self that is hungry, but it's always hungry for
something or someone.

DM: It is either object-related or it is narcissistic relating.

JF: But even in the narcissistic relating, it is object relating of a
kind.

DM: That's right, yes, it doesn't apprehend the id and the superego and evaluate itself in those terms, it evaluates itself
experientially in terms of relationship. Where the relationship is narcissistic, it apprehends itself as part of a gang of
children in opposition to the parents. When it is related to
the parents, it experiences the obsessional situation where
the parents are separated and are related to separately. Or
it relates to them as a combined object and apprehends
itself in its dependence and its inferiority to this combined
object.

JF: Then with this sense of identity, this infantile sense of
identity, there are certain anxieties.

DM: Yes. In Freudian terms they would be classified as superego anxieties. In Kleinian terms there is also the question of

ego-ideal anxieties, which are mainly feelings of dependence, feelings of regret.

JF: In Kleinian terms, in terms of the paranoid–schizoid position, are those anxieties then primary in terms of the infantile situation?

DM: Yes. And they are dependent on the qualities of the internal
object and the qualities of relationship to them, and that is
the core of the personality.

JF: So, if that's our starting point—the infantile sense of identity—one other characteristic is that they are very—shall we
say—fleeting or momentary, or fragmentary. They're not
organized into some stable sense of the self.

DM: Well, the trouble is that there is such instability, which is
dependent on the external world context. As I say, when
you're in a group, they disappear. When the current relationships have very little intimate quality, they are largely
paranoid–schizoid.

JF: And in terms of an infantile sense of identity, the kind of
relating seems to me to be characterized by intimacy, but of
an unstable kind. It might be intimate at one moment and
not at the next.

DM: Yes, quite. The relationship to the parents varies from being
experienced in an aristocratic mode, for instance, or experienced in the obsessional mode of omnipotently controlling
and separating these objects. Or it can be in a very paranoid mode, where these objects are still so mixed up with
projected parts of the self that they don't function as
objects, but function as what are sometimes called "self-
objects".

JF: So, it's at this point, where anxieties associated with the
infantile sense of identity become overwhelming, that one
sees the kind of narcissistic identifications, as a defence
against those anxieties?

DM: Well, I don't know if they are a defence against, or whether
they are just a fact of the level of relationship and a level of
intimacy to one's internal objects.

JF: Descriptively it almost looks as if one moves through a

spectrum that starts with infantile sense of identity to a kind of narcissistic identification and then hopefully beyond that, but one almost has to move through that stage of the organization of the self in these narcissistic ways.

DM: Yes, there tends to be, as seen in analysis, this cyclical process. One sees it in the session, one sees it in the week, one sees it in the term of analysis—this cyclical process that only spirals forward in its development very slowly.

JF: Then one might also see it in the adult couple relationship, that is, moving through a similar kind of cycle, where the partner becomes a kind of transference object and there may be infantile identifications, there may be narcissistic identifications.

DM: Yes, quite.

JF: One of the main points you highlight is that when we move to a narcissistic identification, the sense of identity is delusional, while there's something genuine—or, shall we say, spontaneous—about the infantile sense of identity.

DM: The projective type of narcissism results in a delusional sense of identity, of really *being* the object. That's the grandiosity and that gives way very quickly to claustrophobia.

JF: It seems to me that one could say that a lot of the discussion about projective narcissistic identification talks about what part of the self or internal object is projected, whereas it seems to me you also talk about a different perspective, which I think one could call "phenomenological". That is, you describe the phenomenology of the narcissistic state of mind, the person who is in projective identification has certain characteristics of that state of mind.

DM: Yes, and the predominant characteristic is that it's a different world, the world inside the object, which has a strong resemblance to the political world outside.

JF: And being in that other world also produces characteristic states of mind, like certainty or arrogance.

DM: The whole spectrum of grandiosity.

JF: The reason I think that's important is that sometimes one might, with a patient, or with a couple, see a certain state of mind, a kind of grandiosity, a kind of arrogance, without being able to say what's being projected into whom. That is, you might not be able to describe the dynamics of it, but you could describe the phenomenology of the appearance, that this person seems to be of this state of mind.

DM: That's right. I think you can describe the geography of it.

JF: Yes. You're defining the geography by describing the state of mind.

DM: When you see certain states of mind, you can be fairly sure that you're seeing a variance in the geography.

JF: Yes, but when you hear a dream, you might have some idea of the shape and the contours of that geography.

DM: That's right, yes.

JF: But you seem to be doing something important, which is to help us to stop and observe the state of mind that may be prior to our hearing the dreams or having some idea what the contours of that geography are like.

DM: They're the sort of thing you can see in the patient's face as the patient comes in.

JF: And you can see in the way the couple interact with each other, the tone of voice, the kind of arrogance and so on. Another thing you say—which I wonder if you could say a bit more about—is that in these projective identifications there is always a sense of damage to the object. Is that because of the sense of an uninvited entry?

DM: Yes, it seems to me that the object in that case is always parasitized. Therefore, that projective mode is seldom very far from hypochondria.

JF: And at the same time the state of mind of an intrusive entry into an object upon which one becomes parasitic can vary.

DM: Well, I think that in the case of projective identification, it depends very much on the compartment [of the internal mother's body] that you get into. If you get into the head/breast, you get into the personality and identify it with the personality of the object. In the case of other compartments, one is much more identified with the goings on, as it were, in these other compartments. It's much more evidently a social situation.

JF: What effect does that have on the state of mind then—that one's interested in the goings on?

DM: In the case of being in the rectum [of the internal mother], then you get the political aspects of the social environment. In the case of the genital projection, you get the continual eroticization of everything.

JF: When you use the term "political" in that situation, some people might say that it's a pejorative use of the word "political".

DM: Yes, well, it probably is a pejorative use of the word "political", because to my mind politics have to do solely really with survival, and they are absolutely egocentric.

JF: So if we define the state of mind and this political state of mind and don't use the word "political", we would talk about it in terms of a state of mind concerned only with survival.

DM: That's how it comes across to me, yes.

JF: Whereas in the genital area eroticization means that there is a continuous state of excitement.

DM: Yes, the garden of earthly pleasures.

JF: How would that be connected with your widened sense of masturbation, which means a use of the body to generate an omnipotent state of mind? Is that connected with this eroticization, this excitement?

DM: It seems to me that the distinction between excitement and emotion is very central to this. Masturbation generates excitement, it doesn't generate emotion.

JF: How would you distinguish between excitement and emotion?

DM: The thing about excitement is that it is whipped up, it is lacking authenticity.

JF: So it might be possible to be quite confused between excitement and emotion. Unless one had had some real experience of emotion, would one know the difference?

DM: Of course, it's my contention that almost everybody has had those sort of experiences which, to my mind, are the experience of the aesthetic object.

JF: I'm not sure that everyone would have a sense of differentiation between excitement and emotion. I can think of patients I have seen, where excitement is what they mean by emotion.

DM: Yes, but my contention is that it has been had and lost— that this differentiation has been lost, and that emotion has been abandoned in favour of excitement.

JF: Or could we say that this differentiation, this distinction, is defensively attacked and destroyed? A kind of defensive view that excitement is available as a substitute, a defence against emotion that feels intolerable?

DM: The "attacked and destroyed" seems to me to apply to the perversities and to what I think of as the negative grid. There is a whole process for generating lies and self-deception and so on. It may succeed in destroying the differentiation, but I don't think always.

JF: And, indeed, "lost" means it is recoverable?

DM: I think so, yes.

JF: It must be part of the pathos of that state of mind that people have a sense of the hollowness of it.

DM: It's my impression—perhaps with the exception of psychopaths, which seem a very special group really, whom I think of as people who are busy projecting their paranoia.

JF: To look again then at the question of intimacy and the question of this narcissistic or projective identification state of mind—what sort of intimacy is possible, then? What is the nature of the intimacy? Or is there none?

DM: No, I think projective identification precludes intimacy. Even in the head/breast identification it's omniscient and controlling and possessive and so on. It hasn't a shred of intimacy about it.

JF: But if there is a kind of process between two people, for example, where there is something like a mutual projective identification, a fitting-in to someone else's projections, then there's something that might look like intimacy but would be more like collusion.

DM: Yes, it's something that grows up between siblings very frequently. It grows up slowly and gradually, is adjusted to fit, and then of course that sibling situation may be repeated in a later relationship of either a "doll's-house" type or various kinds of sadomasochistic relationships.

JF: If the sense of identity is delusional, could we then talk about a *delusion of intimacy*?

DM: Yes, the masochists often claim to be deeply in love with the sadists—and believe it.

JF: This kind of delusion of intimacy would have the same relationship to intimacy as the delusion of identity has to the infantile sense of identity. It resembles in some way that which is genuine.

DM: Well, it's based on this loss of differentiation between emotion and excitement. Delusion of benevolence, for instance, is one of the most difficult things to disentangle.

JF: Why is it so difficult to disentangle?

DM: Because it usually finds objects that are greatly gratified by it.

JF: But it can't include the concern for the object of the depressive position.

DM: It almost always eventually results in disillusionment and the discovery of the parasitism—they're so ungrateful.

JF: The person who has this kind of delusion of benevolence is actually parasitic on the object.

DM: In a sense it's a mutual parasitism.

JF: In that sense, for example, the sadomasochistic relationship is parasitic.

DM: Yes. Of course, what you hear from patients so often seems to be of the "nobody-loves-me" variety. But what you actually discover in analysis is what poor acceptors of love people are—that they hold it at arm's length, they look at its teeth to see if they're too long—a gift horse in the mouth.

JF: I'd like to end by asking you about what I think is a

particularly important, even radical, view about the of the adult part of the self, the achievement of what one might call an "adult sense of identity". You linked this intimately with introjective identification, in particular introjective identification with the combined object. It suggests that in one way dependence is at the heart of the human experience because in the end we are dependent on our internal objects.

DM: Quite right. And they are either apprehended on account of their superego functions, or they are apprehended primarily on the basis of their ego-ideal functions. And it is the latter that gives stability to the personality.

JF: It gives stability because there can be a kind of aspiration.

DM: That's right, it generates feelings of unworthiness and inferiority, which generates growth and development.

JF: A particular sense of unworthiness—not the kind of unworthiness that one would get in a paranoid–schizoid state of mind, where there's a kind of hopelessness, but a kind of unworthiness that includes striving to emulate the object.

DM: Yes, it grows out of appreciation, gratitude, and recognition that you have been treated according to your needs and not according to your worth. This is the essence of the good parental position—responding to the child's neediness.

JF: In a way this narcissistic state of mind is an attempt to have arrived, whereas this introjective identification state of mind is recognition that one never arrives, but one is always striving.

DM: That's right. That one's internal objects are always ahead of you in their development and therefore in a position to teach you—and the growing person is constantly finding new teachers.

JF: And the growing person may also seek to find a loving partner, a relationship with another that has these qualities of humility, of unworthiness, of striving.

DM: It seems more than likely.

JF: It's almost a way of defining the intimate relationship of the adult couple—to be in that state of mind.

DM: Yes, that there is some sort of reverberation that has to do with relating to one another's internal objects. And it is my view of the transference that the analyst offers a share of his internal objects to his patients, and the transference is to his internal objects.

JF: Known through the relationship with the analyst?

DM: Well, experienced, experienced with the analyst as the priest or mouth-piece of these internal objects—not claiming to have these qualities for himself.

JF: That would be again not only a definition of the analytic situation, but could also be a way of understanding the adult intimate loving relationship.

DM: And the humility towards one another that's involved.

JF: And the treating each other according to need comes into that, the parental function?

DM: Yes.

JF: Thank you very much, Dr Meltzer.

REFERENCES

Bick, E. (1968). The experience of the skin in early object relations. *International Journal of Psychoanalysis*, *49*, 484–486. Also in M. Harris Williams (Ed.), *Collected Papers of Martha Harris and Esther Bick*. Perthshire, Scotland: Clunie Press.

Bion, W. R. (1958). On arrogance. In: *Second Thoughts*. London: Heinemann. [Reprinted London: Karnac Books, 1984.]

Bion, W. R. (1959). Attacks on linking. In: *Second Thoughts*. London: Heinemann. [Reprinted London: Karnac Books, 1984.]

Bion, W. R. (1962a). *Learning from Experience*. London: Heinemann Medical. [Reprinted London: Karnac Books, 1984.]

Bion, W. R. (1962b). A theory of thinking. In: *Second Thoughts*. London: Heinemann. [Reprinted London: Karnac Books, 1984.]

Bion, W. R. (1970). *Attention and Interpretation*. London: Tavistock. [Reprinted London: Karnac Books, 1984.]

Bion, W. R. (1990). *Brazilian Lectures*. London: Karnac Books.

Brenman Pick, I. (1985). Working through in the countertransference. *International Journal of Psycho-Analysis*, *66*, 157–166.

Britton, R. (1989). The missing link: parental sexuality in the Oedipus complex. In: J. Steiner (Ed.), *The Oedipus Complex Today: Clinical Implications* (pp. 83–101). London: Karnac Books.

Britton, R. (1992a). Keeping things in mind. In: R. Anderson (Ed.), *Clinical Lectures on Klein and Bion* (pp. 102–113). London: Routledge.

Britton, R. (1992b). The Oedipus situation and the depressive position. In: R. Anderson (Ed.), *Clinical Lectures on Klein and Bion* (pp. 34–45). London: Routledge.

Cleavely, E. (1993). Relationships: interaction, defences, and transformations. In: S. Ruszczynski (Ed.), *Psychotherapy with Couples* (pp. 56–59). London: Karnac Books.

Colman, W. (1993). Marriage as a psychological container. In: S. Ruszczynski (Ed.), *Psychotherapy with Couples* (pp. 70–96). London: Karnac Books.

Dicks, H. (1967). *Marital Tensions*. London: Routledge & Kegan Paul. [Reprinted London: Karnac Books, 1993.]

Feldman, M. (1989). The Oedipus complex: manifestations in the inner world and the therapeutic situation. In: J. Steiner (Ed.), *The Oedipus Complex Today: Clinical Implications* (pp. 103–128). London: Karnac Books.

Feldman, M. (1994). Projective identification in phantasy and enactment. *Psychoanalytic Inquiry, 14* (3), 423–440.

Feldman, M. & Spillius, E. Bott (Eds.) (1989). *Psychic Equilibrium and Psychic Change: Selected Papers of Betty Joseph*. London: Tavistock/Routledge.

Fisher, J. (1993). The impenetrable other: ambivalence and the Oedipal conflict in work with couples. In: S. Ruszczynski (Ed.), *Psychotherapy with Couples* (pp. 142–166). London: Karnac Books.

Fisher, J. (1994). Intrusive identification, the claustrum and the couple. *Journal of the British Association of Psychotherapists, 27* (Summer), 3–19.

Freud, S. (1910c). Leonardo da Vinci and a memory of his childhood. In: *Standard Edition, 11* (pp. 59–137). London: Hogarth Press.

Freud, S. (1914d). On narcissism: an introduction. In: *Standard Edition, 14* (pp. 67–102). London: Hogarth Press.

Heimann, P. (1952). Certain functions of introjection and projection in early infancy. In: M. Klein, P. Heimann, S. Isaacs, & J. Riviere (Eds.), *Developments in Psycho-Analysis* (pp. 122–168). London: Hogarth Press. [Reprinted London: Karnac Books, 1989.]

Hinshelwood, R. D. (1991). *A Dictionary of Kleinian Thought*. London: Free Association Press.

Joseph, B. (1979). Projective identification: some clinical aspects. In: E. Bott Spillius & M. Feldman (Eds.), *Psychic Equilibrium and Psychic Change: Selected Papers of Betty Joseph* (pp. 168–180). London: Routledge.

Joseph, B. (1985). Transference: the total situation. In: E. Bott Spillius & M. Feldman (Eds.), *Psychic Equilibrium and Psychic Change: Selected Papers of Betty Joseph* (pp. 156–167). London: Routledge, 1989.

Joseph, B. (1987). Projective identification: some clinical aspects. In: E. Bott Spillius & M. Feldman (Eds.), *Psychic Equilibrium and Psychic Change: Selected Papers of Betty Joseph* (pp. 168–180). London: Routledge, 1989.

Jung, C. G. (1925). Marriage as a psychological relationship. In: *Collected Works. Vol. 17* (pp. 324–345). London: Routledge and Kegan Paul.

Klein, M. (1946). Notes on some schizoid mechanisms. In: *The Writings of Melanie Klein, Vol. III* (pp. 1–24). London: Hogarth Press, 1975. [Reprinted London: Karnac Books, 1993.]

Klein, M. (1952a). The origins of transference. In: *Envy and Gratitude and Other Works: The Writings of Melanie Klein, Vol. III* (pp. 48–56). London: Hogarth Press. [Reprinted London: Karnac Books, 1993.]

Klein, M. (1952b). Notes on some schizoid mechanisms. In: M. Klein, P. Heimann, S. Isaacs, & J. Riviere (Eds.), *Developments in Psycho-Analysis* (pp. 292–320). London: Hogarth Press. [Reprinted London: Karnac Books, 1989.]

Klein, M. (1955). On identification. In: M. Klein, P. Heimann, & R. Money-Kyrle, *New Directions in Psycho-Analysis* (pp. 309–345). London: Tavistock. [Reprinted London: Karnac Books, 1977.]

Klein, M. (1959). Our adult world and its roots in infancy. In: *Envy and Gratitude and Other Works. The Writings of Melanie Klein, Vol. 3* (pp. 247–263). London: Hogarth Press, 1975. [Reprinted London: Karnac Books, 1993.]

Lyons, A., & Mattinson, J. (1993). Individuation in marriage. In: S. Ruszczynski (Ed.), *Psychotherapy with Couples* (pp. 104–125). London: Karnac Books.

Meltzer, D. (1971/1994). Sincerity: a study in the atmosphere of human relations. In: A. Hahn (Ed), *Sincerity and Other Works: Collected Papers of Donald Meltzer* (pp. 185–284). London: Karnac Books, 1994.

Meltzer, D. (1973). On routine and inspired interpretations. In: A. Hahn (Ed.), *Sincerity and Other Works: Collected Papers of Donald Meltzer* (pp. 458–468). London: Karnac Books, 1994.

Meltzer, D. (1976). The delusion of clarity of insight. In: *The Claustrum: An Investigation of Claustrophobic Phenomena* (pp. 74–85). Perthshire, Scotland: Clunie Press.

Meltzer, D. (1978). A note on introjective processes. In: A. Hahn (Ed.), *Sincerity and Other Works: Collected Papers of Donald Meltzer* (pp. 458–468). London: Karnac Books, 1994.

Meltzer, D. (1986). *Studies in Extended Metapsychology: Clinical Applications of Bion's Ideas.* Perthshire, Scotland: Clunie Press.

Meltzer, D. (1992). *The Claustrum: An Investigation of Claustrophobic Phenomena.* Perthshire, Scotland: Clunie Press.

Meltzer, D. (1994). *Sincerity and Other Works: Collected Papers of Donald Meltzer.* (Ed. A. Hahn). London: Karnac Books, 1994.

Meltzer, D., et al. (1982). The conceptual difference between projective identification (Klein) and container–contained (Bion). In: *Studies in Extended Metapsychology: Clinical Applications of Bion's Ideas* (pp. 50–69). Perthshire, Scotland: Clunie Press, 1986.

Meltzer, D., & Harris Williams, M. (1988). *The Apprehension of Beauty.* Perthshire, Scotland: Clunie Press.

O'Shaughnessy, E. (1988). W. R. Bion's theory of thinking and new techniques in child analysis. In: E. Bott Spillius (Ed.), *Melanie Klein Today. Vol. 2: Mainly Practice* (pp. 177–190). London: Routledge, 1988.

O'Shaughnessy, E. (1989). The invisible Oedipus complex. In: J. Steiner (Ed.), *The Oedipus Complex Today: Clinical Implications* (pp. 129–150). London: Karnac Books.

O'Shaughnessy, E. (1993). *Remnant Couples.* Unpublished paper.

Pincus, L. (Ed.) (1960). *Marriage: in Emotional Conflict and Growth.* London: Institute of Marital Studies.

Rey, H. (1979). Schizoid phenomena in the borderline. In: J. LeBoit and A. Capponi (Eds.), *Advances in the Psychotherapy of the Borderline Patient* (pp. 449–484). New York: Jason Aronson. [Reprinted in: H. Rey, *Universals of Psychoanalysis in the Treat-*

ment of Psychotic and Borderline States (Jean Magagna, ed.) (pp. 8–30). London: Free Association Books, 1994.]

Rosenfeld, H. (1964). On the psychopathology of narcissism: a clinical approach. *International Journal of Psycho-Analysis, 45,* 169–179. Also in *Psychotic States.* London: Hogarth Press, 1965. [Reprinted London: Karnac Books, 1985.]

Rosenfeld, H. (1965). *Psychotic States.* London: Hogarth Press. [Reprinted London: Karnac Books, 1985.]

Rosenfeld, H. (1971). A clinical approach to the psycho-analytical theory of the life and death instincts: an investigation into the aggressive aspects of narcissism. *International Journal of Psycho-Analysis, 52,* 169–178.

Rosenfeld, H. (1983). Primitive object relations and mechanisms. *International Journal of Psycho-Analysis, 64,* 261–267.

Rosenfeld, H. (1987). *Impasse and Interpretation.* London: Tavistock Publications.

Ruszczynski, S. (1992). Some notes towards a psychoanalytic understanding of the couple relationship. *Psychoanalytic Psychotherapy, 6* (1), 33–48.

Ruszczynski, S. (Ed.) (1993). *Psychotherapy with Couples.* London: Karnac Books.

Sandler, J. (1976). Countertransference and role responsiveness. *International Revue of Psycho-Analysis, 3,* 43–47.

Sandler, J. (1987). The concept of projective identification. In: *Projection, Identification, Projective Identification* (pp. 13–26). Madison, CT: International Universities Press. London: Karnac Books, 1988.

Segal, H. (1977). Counter-transference. In: *The Work of Hanna Segal* (pp. 81–88). New York: Jason Aronson, 1981. [Reprinted London: Karnac Books, 1986.]

Segal, H. (1983). Some clinical implications of Melanie Klein's work. *International Journal of Psycho-Analysis, 64,* 269–276.

Segal, H. (1989). Preface. In: E. Bott Spillius & M. Feldman (Eds.), *Psychic Equilibrium and Psychic Change: Selected Papers of Betty Joseph* (pp. vii–ix). London: Routledge.

Singer, I. B. (1979). *In My Father's Court.* London: Penguin Books.

Spillius, E. Bott (1988a). General introduction. In: *Melanie Klein Today, Vol. 1: Mainly Theory* (pp. 1–7). London: Routledge.

Spillius, E. Bott (1988b). Introduction. In: E. Bott Spillius (Ed.),

150   REFERENCES

Melanie Klein Today, Vol. 1: Mainly Theory (pp. 81–86). London: Routledge.

Spillius, E. Bott (1992). Clinical experiences of projective identification. In: R. Anderson (Ed.), *Clinical Lectures on Klein and Bion* (pp. 59–73). London: Routledge.

Spillius, E. Bott (1994). Developments in Kleinian thought: overview and personal view. *Psychoanalytic Inquiry, 14,* (3), 324–364.

Steiner, J. (1993). *Psychic Retreats.* London: Routledge.

Tustin, F. (1986). *Autistic Barriers in Neurotic Patients.* London: Karnac Books.

Winnicott, D. W. (1951). Transitional objects and transitional phenomena. In: *Collected Papers: Through Paediatrics to Psycho-Analysis* (pp. 229–242). London: Tavistock, 1958. [Reprinted London: Karnac Books, 1991.]

Winnicott, D. W. (1956). Primary maternal preoccupation. In *Collected Papers: Through Paediatrics to Psycho-Analysis* (pp. 300–305). London: Tavistock, 1958. [Reprinted London: Karnac Books, 1991.]

Winnicott, D. W. (1960a). The theory of the parent/infant relationship. In *The Maturational Processes and the Facilitating Environment* (pp. 37–55). London: Hogarth Press, 1965. [Reprinted London: Karnac Books, 1990.]

Winnicott, D. W. (1960b). Ego distortion in terms of true and false self. In *The Maturational Processes and the Facilitating Environment* (pp. 140–152). London: Hogarth Press, 1965. [Reprinted London: Karnac Books, 1990.]

Winnicott, D. W. (1963). From dependence towards independence in the development of the individual. In: *The Maturational Processes and the Facilitating Environment* (pp. 83–92). London: Hogarth Press, 1965. [Reprinted London: Karnac Books, 1990.]

Winnicott, D. W. (1967). The location of cultural experience. In: *Playing and Reality* (pp. 112–121). London: Tavistock, 1971.

Winnicott, D. W. (1969). The use of an object and relating through identifications. *International Journal of Psycho-Analysis, 50,* 711–716.

INDEX

151